ALASKA

HIGH ROADS TO ADVENTURE

Prepared by the Special Publications Division
National Geographic Society, Washington, D. C.

ALASKA: HIGH ROADS TO ADVENTURE
Photographed by GEORGE F. MOBLEY,
  National Geographic Photographer
Introduction by GILBERT M. GROSVENOR
WILLIAM R. GRAY, NOEL GROVE, JOSEPH JUDGE,
  FRED KLINE, CYNTHIA RUSS RAMSAY,
  Contributing Authors

Published by
THE NATIONAL GEOGRAPHIC SOCIETY
ROBERT E. DOYLE, *President*
MELVIN M. PAYNE, *Chairman of the Board*
GILBERT M. GROSVENOR, *Editor*
MELVILLE BELL GROSVENOR, *Editor-in-Chief*

Prepared by
THE SPECIAL PUBLICATIONS DIVISION
ROBERT L. BREEDEN, *Editor*
DONALD J. CRUMP, *Associate Editor*
PHILIP B. SILCOTT, *Senior Editor*
WILLIAM R. GRAY, *Managing Editor*
TONI EUGENE, TEE LOFTIN, LUCY E. TOLAND,
  Research

Illustrations and Design
STEVE RAYMER, *Picture Editor*
URSULA PERRIN VOSSELER, *Art Director*
SUEZ KEHL, *Design Assistant*
MARIE BRADBY, TONI EUGENE, FRED KLINE,
  TEE LOFTIN, CYNTHIA RUSS RAMSAY,
  JENNIFER URQUHART, *Picture Legends*
JOHN D. GARST, JR., ISKANDAR BADAY,
  CHARLES W. BERRY, MARGARET A. DEANE,
  ALFRED L. ZEBARTH, LEO B. ZEBARTH, *Maps*

Production and Printing
ROBERT W. MESSER, *Production Manager*
GEORGE V. WHITE, *Assistant Production Manager*
RAJA D. MURSHED, JUNE L. GRAHAM,
  CHRISTINE A. ROBERTS, *Production Assistants*
JOHN R. METCALFE, *Engraving and Printing*
JANE H. BUXTON, STEPHANIE S. COOKE,
  MARY C. HUMPHREYS, SUZANNE J.
  JACOBSON, CLEO PETROFF, MARILYN L.
  WILBUR, LINDA M. YEE, *Staff Assistants*
BARBARA L. KLEIN, *Index*

Library of Congress ⅭⅠⅤ Data: page 199

*Whiskered giants, walruses drift in Bristol Bay on
the southwest coast of Alaska—home for a wide
range of wildlife. Overleaf: A halo of clouds
brushes the rumpled flank of 16,390-foot Mount
Blackburn in the Wrangell Mountains. Page 1:
On the Aleutian Island of Unalaska, a beaming
Native girl feeds a pet sea lion pup. Bookbinding:
Alaska's state symbols—Sitka spruce, willow
ptarmigan, forget-me-not, king salmon.*

PAGE 1: NATIONAL GEOGRAPHIC PHOTOGRAPHER GORDON W. GAHAN;
BOOKBINDING: CHARLES W. BERRY

CONTENTS

A New Future for America's Northern Star 6

NATIONAL GEOGRAPHIC PHOTOGRAPHER BRUCE DALE

A New Future for America's

TWO DECADES AGO, on my first journey to Alaska, I flew into Anchorage on a cloudless summer day. The sleepy city of several thousand people basked in the sun, tranquil and unhurried. Compared with the surrounding grandeur of sparkling Cook Inlet and the snow-touched Chugach Mountains, it seemed perilously insignificant—a tiny enclave of mankind engulfed by a vast wilderness.

Today, I am astonished at the changes I find in Alaska. Anchorage has become a metropolis of skyscrapers and shopping malls—and tens of thousands of people. The airport is continually thronged with tourists and business people, and downtown traffic jams are common. Somehow, the city's natural backdrop has been diminished. Urban sprawl and Anchorage itself—not the water or the peaks—have become the dominant features of the landscape.

The growing pains of Anchorage are but a reflection of forces working throughout the state. Today, dramatic changes are sweeping through Alaska, bringing radical shifts in population, the economic structure, and the social order.

Because of these shifts, Alaska is poised at a crossroads and is facing several decisions: how best to develop its extensive mineral resources; how best to preserve the wild beauty of its land and to protect the unique character of its wildlife; how best to achieve equality among its small but diverse citizenry; how best to fit into the mainstream of American life; how best to handle the explosive problems of increasing population, increasing crime, and increasing shortages of housing and other services. Within the next handful of years, the direction that the state will take on each of these issues will be evident; the face of Alaska may change dramatically depending on what is decided.

Several forces have been at work over the last decade to bring Alaska to its current delicate position.

The first—and perhaps the major—force is oil. The discovery of reserves of black gold in 1968 on the North Slope at Prudhoe Bay brought a bonanza of wealth and a burden of problems. Specialized technology was developed to tap the oil and to transport it from the frozen expanse of the Arctic to the ice-free port of Valdez on Prince William Sound. Development of the oil resource and construction of the 800-mile trans-Alaska pipeline have brought riches, corruption, and hordes of people to a frontier state little prepared for them.

Another force matured in 1971 with the passage of the Alaska Native

Mellow light of the midnight sun touches barren crags in the Brooks Range and burnishes their reflection in a mountain pond. Gates of the Arctic, a proposed national park, envelops 8.4 million acres in this wilderness area. The Federal Government has designated vast stretches of Alaska's land for inclusion within new national parks, national forests, wildlife refuges, and wild rivers.

6

Northern Star

By Gilbert M. Grosvenor

Claims Settlement Act by the Federal Government. This single law brought a sweeping new alignment of land, power, and money to the state. Under the provisions of the act, Alaska's Natives — Aleuts, Eskimos, and Indians — were awarded nearly a billion dollars in revenues, and granted title to 40 million acres of land, land that their peoples had historically claimed as their own.

A dozen Native-owned regional corporations and more than 200 smaller village corporations were established to administer and to develop the new holdings. While recompensing the Natives for what was rightfully theirs, the act deprived Alaska of a large chunk of public domain and also caused resentment among some of the white citizens.

The carving up of Alaska's land has taken another controversial form. The Federal Government has proposed 83 million acres for inclusion within new or expanded national parks, national forests, national wildlife refuges, and wild and scenic rivers. The state government, disputing these proposals, hopes to place some of these areas under its own jurisdiction. And private interests — the mining and timbering industries among them — are lobbying to keep some tracts of this acreage available for development of resources. Congress established a deadline of December 1978 to settle the fate of Alaska's land.

Long an emotional subject, this issue has provoked heated conflicts between conservationist and developer, wildlife preservationist and trophy hunter, private citizen and government bureaucrat.

Myriad other forces — some spin-offs or by-products of these three major ones — are also affecting the State of Alaska today. Offshore oil development, natural-gas pipelines, a grossly inflated economy, over-burdened living facilities and social services, and the need for quicker transportation of people and freight from the Lower Forty-Eight all are problems which Alaska must confront in the next few years. In the chapters of this book, many of these issues will be explained and exemplified. The final chapter will look to the future.

On my first trip to Alaska I found a wilderness land that seemed untroubled by the familiar pressures weighing down the rest of the nation. On subsequent visits, I discovered that Alaskans were being forced to catch up — and catch up quickly — with the pulsebeat of America. Even the Alaska Highway — the overland route linking the Lower Forty-Eight to Alaska — has begun to change, as you will discover in the next chapter. Years ago, I drove it as a winding gravel track; today, it is gradually being straightened and paved.

While I accept the justifications for paving such a wilderness route — or of logging a majestic forest or building a hotel at a spot of untrammeled beauty — I still mourn the passing of any element that makes Alaska — at least in my mind — the last great frontier.

Glowing sparks blossom from a worker's torch as he welds a steel beam for a piling at Valdez, southern end of the trans-Alaska pipeline. The discovery of oil at Prudhoe Bay catapulted Alaska into a new era, bringing people, money, and technology to the north. Environmental conflict, social change, and economic problems have added to the burden of a state seeking its future.

1/Alaska Highway: Winding

"YOU ALL SET BACK THERE?"

Perched on the driver's seat, burly Ron Morton tossed the question to me over his shoulder. He braced his feet, widespread, against the top of the wagon box, and pulled back hard on two sets of lines, barely holding in check the team of four Thoroughbreds trembling with eagerness.

It had been a long winter, and their blood rose like the sap that greened the trees around Ron's barn and corral. Born to run with jockeys on their backs, they were now being trained under harness for one of British Columbia's most popular spectator sports—chuck-wagon racing. "It grew out of the old roundup days, when cooks of different outfits would race each other to the next day's camp," Ron had explained earlier. "There must be frying pans scattered all over the countryside."

Standing behind the seat, I flexed my knees and tightly held one of the iron hoops supporting the wagon's canvas cover. "I'm ready!"

"HYAAH!" The Thoroughbreds bolted, snapping the small wagon forward and throwing me hard against the iron hoop. Immediately, we were careering down a narrow wagon trail behind the barn, with Ron sawing at the lines, leaning back to control the horses. Their plunging backs and the metal harness connections made music as pickets of white poplars flashed by in a stroboscopic blur.

For the next ten minutes, I was an alertly excited passenger in a lurching, noisy anachronism. What a strange conveyance, I reflected later, in a world of purring automobiles and air-cushioned comfort. Life is a pendulum swinging between past and present along the Alaska Highway, the first—and still the major—overland connection between the far north and the lower part of the North American continent. I have twice traveled the 1,520-mile route from Dawson Creek, British Columbia, to Fairbanks, Alaska. Along the way, I talked with trappers, homesteaders, and merchants who spoke of pioneering, of frontier, of hardship, danger, and isolation—as though it had all happened yesterday. Continually, I was amazed to find that it was nearly so, that yesterday is as recent in this young land as the road that opened its wilderness.

"When I came to this country there wasn't so much as an ax mark where the town now stands," I was told by Walter Taylor of Fort Nelson, British Columbia—one of the settlements along the highway large enough to be called towns. "I ran a barge on the Sikanni Chief River and the Fort Nelson River in '34, stopping wherever Indians and white trappers were, trading goods for furs."

Headlights piercing the mist, a solitary truck grumbles uphill on the Alaska Highway as it meanders through a spruce forest in Canada. The 1,520-mile track—built as a supply road during World War II—stretches between Dawson Creek, British Columbia, and Fairbanks, Alaska; it provides the major overland link between the 49th State and the rest of North America.

Link to the North

By Noel Grove

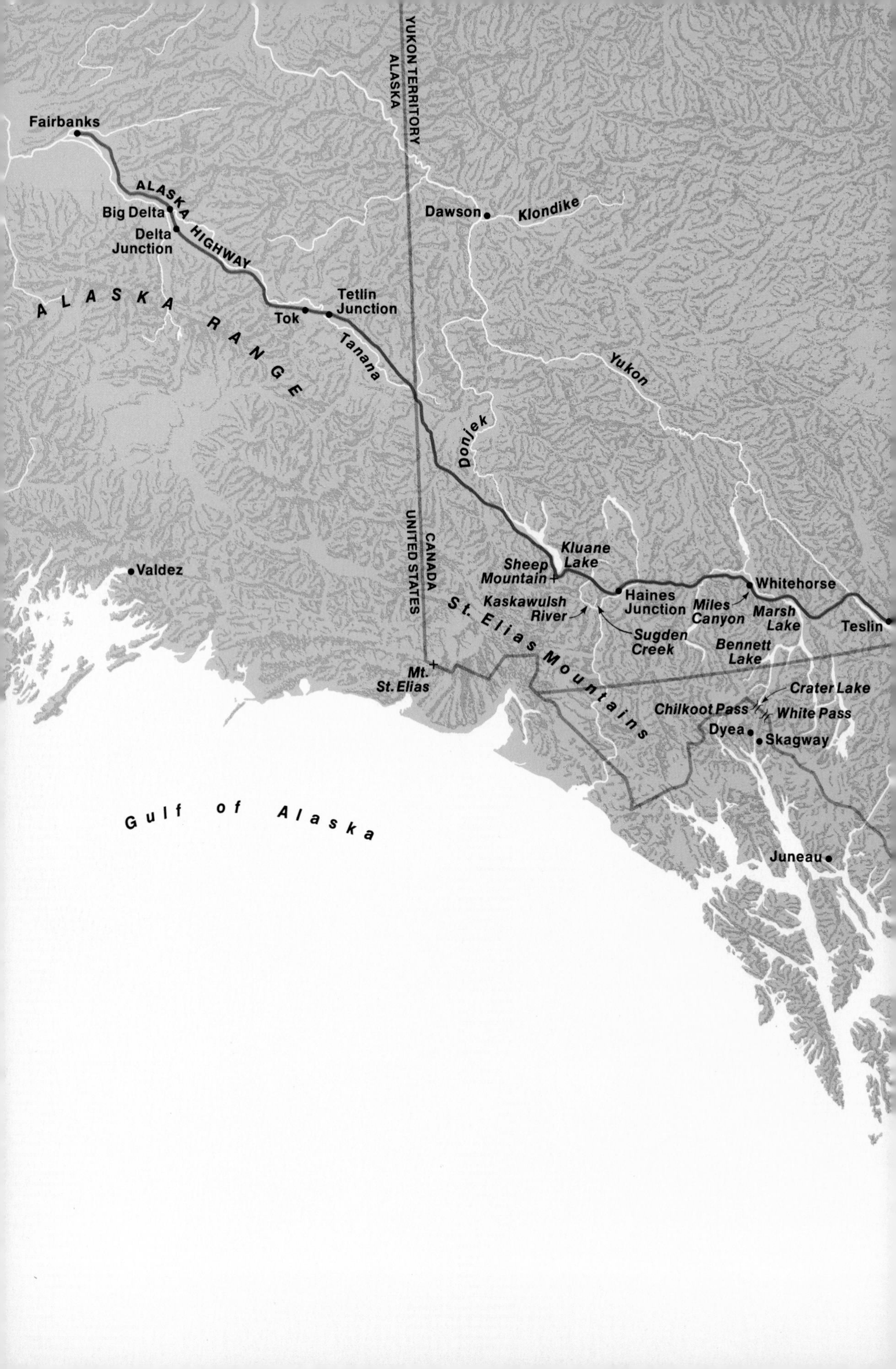

Fairbanks

ALASKA HIGHWAY

Big Delta

Delta
Junction

ALASKA RANGE

A L A S K A   R A N G E

Tok

Tetlin
Junction

Tanana

YUKON TERRITORY
ALASKA

Dawson

Klondike

Yukon

Donjek

CANADA
UNITED STATES

Kluane
Lake

Sheep
Mountain

Kaskawulsh
River

Haines
Junction

Miles
Canyon

Whitehorse

Marsh
Lake

Teslin

Sugden
Creek

Bennett
Lake

Valdez

St. Elias Mountains

S t .   E l i a s   M o u n t a i n s

Mt.
St. Elias

Crater Lake

White Pass

Chilkoot Pass

Dyea

Skagway

Gulf   of   Alaska

Juneau

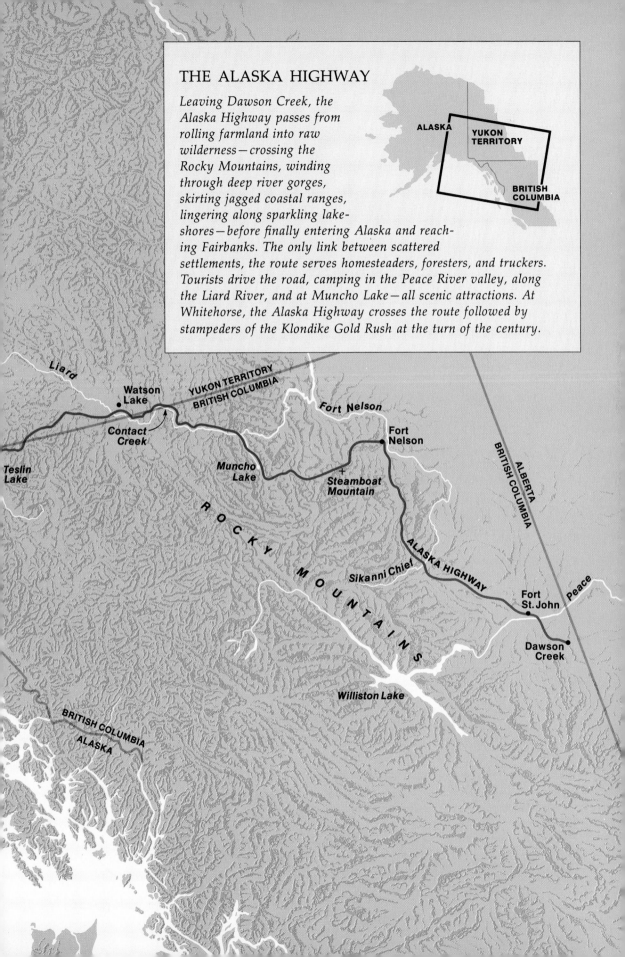

THE ALASKA HIGHWAY

Leaving Dawson Creek, the Alaska Highway passes from rolling farmland into raw wilderness—crossing the Rocky Mountains, winding through deep river gorges, skirting jagged coastal ranges, lingering along sparkling lakeshores—before finally entering Alaska and reaching Fairbanks. The only link between scattered settlements, the route serves homesteaders, foresters, and truckers. Tourists drive the road, camping in the Peace River valley, along the Liard River, and at Muncho Lake—all scenic attractions. At Whitehorse, the Alaska Highway crosses the route followed by stampeders of the Klondike Gold Rush at the turn of the century.

ALASKA

YUKON TERRITORY

BRITISH COLUMBIA

Liard

Watson Lake

YUKON TERRITORY

BRITISH COLUMBIA

Contact Creek

Fort Nelson

Fort Nelson

Teslin Lake

Muncho Lake

Steamboat Mountain

ALBERTA

BRITISH COLUMBIA

R O C K Y   M O U N T A I N S

Sikanni Chief

ALASKA HIGHWAY

Fort St. John

Peace

Dawson Creek

Williston Lake

BRITISH COLUMBIA

ALASKA

And that was a hundred years after Jim Bridger had trapped and traded in the Rocky Mountains south of Canada. In 1934 the population of all Canada barely exceeded ten million, and British Columbia and the Yukon Territory were but sparsely inhabited. Alaska remained a barren tract in the minds of most Americans. Only later did it become fully apparent that "Seward's Folly" was indeed a bargain at $7,200,000 — less than two cents per acre — because of its fish, fur, minerals, and timber.

In the late 1930's, a nation across the Pacific was looking for room to expand. American military leaders became increasingly aware that the far-flung Aleutian Islands reached invitingly to within 750 miles of the north-ernmost Japanese naval base. They suggested that a supply road be built where no permanent road had ever existed, through British Columbia and the Yukon, connecting Alaska with the existing 48 states. Canadian jour-nalist George Murray warned, "We will either build a highway up to Alaska or the Japanese will build it down to us."

With the bombing of Pearl Harbor on December 7, 1941, the road be-came a necessity. Sea and air supply lines to Alaska were vulnerable to submarine attack and bad weather. In the summer of 1942, some 10,000 United States soldiers began work on the road at strategic points between Dawson Creek and Fairbanks, hoping to finish before the year was out. Northland veterans shook their heads and said the Army would be lucky to complete a survey by that time.

Road making, under ideal conditions, is a slow, tedious process of clearing, leveling, grading, and surfacing. It promised to be a nightmare across an untracked wilderness of mountains, mud, and muskegs — bogs of spongy moss and decaying vegetation. Some people predicted that the job would take five or six years — but the war would not permit that. Even as Army bulldozers began clearing a track, Japanese troops bombed Dutch Harbor, a naval base off the island of Unalaska, and landed on three of the other Aleutians. Working around the clock, the big Caterpillar trac-tors, or "cats," and the plows and graders that followed, rammed through a rough truck trail from Dawson Creek to Fairbanks in a little more than six months of concentrated work, an astounding pace of eight miles a day.

Private contractors followed to upgrade the route by widening and graveling, and building more permanent bridges. But with that first "tote road," usable only when winter cold froze the mud, the overland isolation of Alaska was ended. Supplies flowed during the winter of 1942-43 along the so-called Alaskan-Canadian Military Highway, or "Alcan" for short. Soldiers nicknamed it the "Oilcan Highway," for haste sowed a string of fuel drums along the way.

Today the road is officially called the Alaska Highway, although more than three-quarters of it lies in Canada and is maintained by that govern-ment. To those who live along this winding, dusty, mostly graveled thread of history, it is simply called "The Highway." "The Japanese did this part of the country a favor," Gordon Pack, 83, told me as he poked seeds into the warm earth of his garden near Dawson Creek. "Before the highway, there was nothing here but a few settlers and some wagon trails."

With construction of the Alaska Highway, Dawson Creek lost both its isolation and its anonymity; roads began radiating from the town, and more settlers moved in. "In my opinion, this land is still underdeveloped," said rancher Carl Torio, as we rode quarter horses around his 1,500-acre spread in the rich valley of the Peace River. "Good farmland here sells for $300 an acre, cleared of trees. It's even less than that to the north of us. Why don't people come? Believe it or not, they don't know what's out here. We go down to Vancouver and tell people we're from Dawson Creek and they think we travel around by dogsled!"

I met at least one Vancouver couple who understood what Carl and the others had to say. Danny and Diane Cooper have seen an amazing transformation in their three city-born daughters since they moved from a comfortable home in Vancouver to a cabin without running water near Dawson Creek. On the day I drove up to their 5½-acre farm, I found Diane in her garden.

"We didn't like what was happening to our kids in the city," she said, tucking a windblown strand of brown hair behind her ear. "They would come home from school and just plop down in front of the television. And they were learning too much and too quickly about things that should be learned gradually in life.

"I had never lived without running water before," she continued, as we carried buckets from a pond reservoir—called a dugout in Peace River country—to irrigate her beans, peas, and potatoes. "When we came to look at the place after Danny bought it, I stared at the outhouse and said, 'What's that?' But I wouldn't go back to the city now. Our house and yard there was about as big as this garden. And here the kids ride every day and have chores to do. They love it, they're a lot healthier, and they seem to be developing better values."

Danny, who sacrificed supervisory industrial work for a job in maintenance at the Dawson Creek junior college, has not completely adopted country ways. "I like it out here, but I'm afraid I'm one of those plastic people," he told me candidly. "I go for thick carpets and flush toilets. I'll be all right as soon as I get over that."

Comfort, I discovered, is also sacrificed by those who drive the Alaska Highway, for it is rough-surfaced and filled with sharp curves and dips. Nevertheless, more than 250,000 people make the drive each year. "I don't know how many have told me that driving the Alaska Highway has been a longtime ambition," said Don McCartney, a director of the Peace River Alaska Highway Tourist Association in Dawson Creek. "If they ever pave the road, the size of towns like Dawson Creek will double, but the pioneering spirit associated with driving the highway will be gone."

The town's population swelled to 30,000—more than double its present size—when construction began in 1942; tent cities of American soldiers bloomed on surrounding hillsides. A rough road already existed from Dawson Creek to Fort St. John, 50 miles north. Elsewhere, aerial photography often provided the first clues to a logical route for advance ground parties. As usual in the north, old methods mixed with new. "They'd follow an Indian if he could show them a way over the mountains," John Savela, a mechanic on the highway, told me.

The advance party blazed a center line for the bulldozers to follow. Temporary bridges were hurriedly built across rivers and streams. Then came the first of the big cats, ramming straight ahead, knocking down trees and brush. Flanking the lead machine were two more that broadened the trail. Behind them, more cats pushed brush and trees farther out of the way so that graders and culvert makers could complete the rough road. Within the year that followed, the permanent all-weather highway was built.

Work on both the tote road and the all-weather road was plagued by many discomforts. The men who built the initial track—soldiers from the Lower Forty-Eight—found the extreme cold of the north to be a totally unfamiliar experience.

George Burke of Washington, D. C., an electrician with the all-black 95th Engineers, remembers: "We heard we were going to British Columbia and that temperatures would be 30 below zero; I just couldn't imagine that a man could function in that kind of cold, shinnying up a pole and working with his hands. Just living was uncomfortable. But if you paid attention to instructions about how to dress, you could get along all right."

Clouds of mosquitoes dogged the men when the cold did not. Aggravation over the quantity and size of these insects led to exaggeration. A mosquito reportedly landed at a supply camp once and maintenance men pumped 30 gallons of gasoline into it before they discovered it was not a bush plane. Having encountered the huge mosquitoes of Canada and Alaska, I appreciate the sentiment.

A RUGGED ROAD, that first route called for rugged drivers. Steep grades remain today, but the hair-raising track of wartime has been vastly tamed. At Mile 158, a sign now warns, "Steep Hill. Gear Down." In convoy days a similar one read, "Suicide Hill. Prepare to Meet Thy God."

Dan Weber, a homesteader near Fort St. John when the highway was built, hauled supplies for the Army to augment his farm income. Overturned trucks sometimes littered the roadside, he recalled. "It wasn't too bad if you took it slow," said Weber, now retired, at his home in Fort St. John. "I remember going down a steep, muddy hill and having another truck pass me just going like the dickens. When I rounded a curve lower on the hill, there it was, laid over on its side."

Dawson Creek claims to be Mile Zero, or the beginning of the Alaska Highway. Fort St. John once declared that it should have the honor, because of the original rough truck trail between the two towns. According to official Army reports, Fort St. John was the beginning of new roadbuilding, but time, tradition, and modern road maps stand on the side of Dawson Creek.

For me, the Alaska Highway as a unique, historic road starts at neither town, but at Mile 93. Out of Dawson Creek, past Fort St. John, the road is asphalt, a modern highway smoothed and curried into miles-long straightaways and gentle curves. Grazing cattle and tilled fields gradually give way to forests of spruce, jack pine, and poplar.

Then the signs appear: "Slow. Pavement Ends." It was raining lightly the first time I reached this point, and beyond the gleaming blacktop I could see brown sludge. Within a mile, the mucky film toned the lower half of my car. After ten miles it had covered the whole vehicle. Beneath the muck, though, the surface was hard. It is—as the Army proclaimed in

1945 — an all-weather road, a twisting, narrow band of gravel in a continent crisscrossed by superhighways, a route appealing to the traveler who likes a dash of hardship and a taste of history.

My speed immediately dropped upon reaching the graveled portion, which accounts for more than a thousand of the route's 1,520 miles. The spruce and poplar no longer whizzed by the window. And the curves, the many, many curves, slowed me even more. The signs preceding them are blunt, straightforward announcements: "Bad Corner" and "Slow. Very Dangerous Curve." They mean it. A pickup camper in front of me nearly disappeared in a sudden dip in the road, before emerging on the opposite side, cutting a right angle at a sharp bend. "The road makes so many turns that sometimes you wonder if you are going to Alaska or you've been there and are coming back," a veteran trucker told me.

The hardships of the highway, I believe, are exaggerated. Rock missiles tossed by the tires of oncoming vehicles, I had been warned, would give me a "Yukon windshield," one starred and shattered in several places. Choking clouds of dust raised by traffic would hang over the road for minutes on end. A four-wheel-drive vehicle would be necessary to maneuver through the mud on rainy days. Extra food was mandatory for the long stretches between restaurants, and for the unexpected snowstorms that might isolate me on a high pass.

I drove the highway in a sedan and never cracked a windshield. Mud slowed but never trapped me; it only caked my car. Weaving, turning, dodging, creeping, I became part of this frontier road. And it, judging from the mud on my boots and the dust on my dashboard, became part of me. The distances between towns could easily deplete a stomach and a gasoline tank; but roadhouses staggered at an average of about every 50 miles offer gas, beds, and a cafe where the atmosphere is pure country and the soup often homemade.

The dust, although bothersome, did not choke, nor did the snow entrap, thanks to the armada of road graders and water trucks operated by teams of men stationed at intervals along the route. Less than half an hour south of Fort Nelson on a dry day, I entered a billowing dust cloud kicked up by a huge truck loaded with oil-drilling pipe. Here it is, I thought, the famous Alaska Highway dust; I resigned myself to being caught in it for mile after interminable mile. Abruptly, the dust cleared, although the truck still rumbled in front of me. A mile later I discovered what had happened. Gary Dolen stood beside his tank truck as a motorized pump loaded it with about 2,500 gallons of water from a roadside stream. Gary explained that his job is to spray the road to keep the dust down.

"What do you think of the highway?" he asked.

My approval failed to please him. "If you lived here and drove your own car on it all the time, you'd want it paved," he said. "I bought a new pickup and it broke my heart to drive it on this road. You can't keep a paint job because of the rocks."

The days of the twisting, dusty, muddy, rock-throwing original Alaska Highway may be numbered. "Within five years, most of the first 300 miles should be paved," said Dennie Anderson, project manager of more than a thousand miles of roadway in Canada. (Continued on page 24)

Thrusting across the Donjek River in the Yukon, a pontoon bridge built in 1942 awaits a convoy of Army trucks bound for Alaska. When Japanese forces encroached on Alaska and threatened its ocean supply lines, 10,000 U. S. Army troops constructed bridges and cleared a track through the woods and mountains of Canada and Alaska—all in just slightly more than six months of concentrated work. Permafrost, glacial rivers, rocky heights, swamps, mud, and mosquitoes plagued but never halted the workers. Within another year, 14,000 civilian workers had upgraded the Alaskan-Canadian Military Highway to an all-weather gravel road with steel bridges. Today, the Alaska Highway remains a winding, unpaved road for much of its length; a car (upper, right)—one of as many as 900 vehicles a day—stirs a golden haze of dust in the setting sun. Backpackers and hitchhikers—like these on a spur road near Whitehorse—also follow the route north. Eventually, the entire length will be straightened and paved, and vehicles "busted" by the harshness of driving the road will become an increasingly rare sight.

WAYNE TOWRISS (ABOVE); MACBRIDE MUSEUM COLLECTION, YUKON ARCHIVES (ABOVE, LEFT)

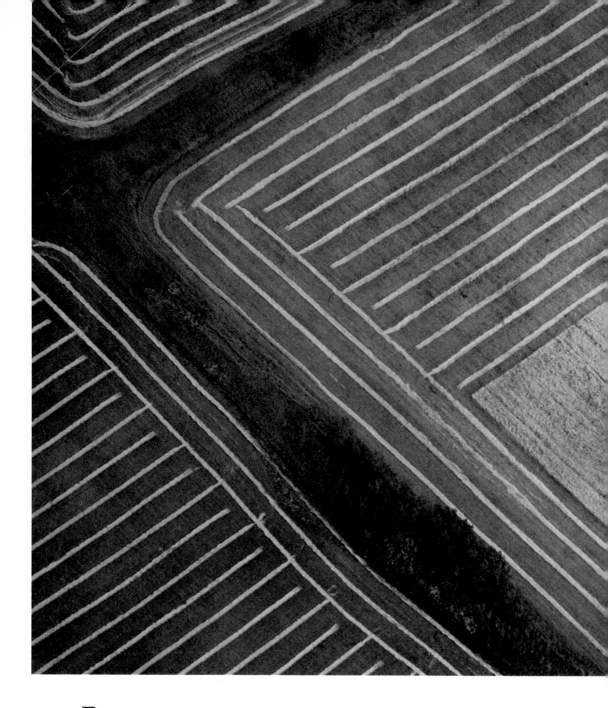

*R*ow by row, ripe barley falls to the harvester on a farm in the Peace River valley near Dawson Creek. In its first miles, the Alaska Highway crosses the western end of this valley, where half a century ago 160-acre tracts of prime farmland went to homesteaders who would settle there and improve the land. "My sons make the third generation to work our farm," says cattle rancher Carl Torio (right), who now owns 1,500 acres near Dawson Creek. From his tractor, Carl watches clover chopped by a forage harvester fill a truck; this silage will help feed his some 600 beef cattle during winter when temperatures can plummet to minus 40° F. "Heavy equipment left over from construction of the Alaska Highway helped us clear this country," Carl said.

*A*mid billows of dust, a chuck wagon rumbles toward the finish line in a rodeo at Dawson

Creek—one of the communities along the Alaska Highway large enough to be called a town.

"But reconstruction and paving of the complete highway could be delayed up to 20 years. We're doing it to get rid of a crooked highway. In summer we get as many as 900 vehicles a day passing a given point. We'll lose some of those who drive it for the adventure, but overall we believe traffic will increase after it's paved and straightened. Little of the new road will be built on the old roadbed; it's just too crooked. When the project is finished, the whole route may be a hundred miles shorter."

But why was the original road built with more loops than a garter snake crawling across a plowed field? The most colorful theory I heard is the anti-strafing strategy. "The Army put in all the curves so an airplane strafing a convoy couldn't wipe out several trucks with one pass," a highway resident told me confidently. That theory has gained romantic popularity, but does not coincide with a history compiled by the Corps of Royal Canadian Engineers: "As speed [of building] was the first consideration the trail was carried around soft spots that might cause delay, detoured around ravines that would have required bridging, and directed towards open country that meant less clearing, thus accounting for much of the crookedness of the road."

Just as towns sprang up along the rivers and railroads of the American West, fledgling communities have feathered out along the Alaska Highway. They have the tentative feel, the air of impermanence of those early frontier towns—with certain modern touches. The floors of hotels creak and give, not from old age but from low-cost construction. Businesses are widely scattered, seemingly without plan—a service station here, a hardware store there, a laundry in between. Poorly constructed houses sprout as though seeded like thistledown. "The new homes here are much different from ours in Europe," observed a hitchhiker from Germany as we drove past a barracks-like cluster in a highway town. "They have no sense of permanence. When we build a home, we build it for our lives, and for our children's lives after us."

The opposite is often true in Alaska Highway towns, according to Fort Nelson's athletic mayor, Andrew Schuck. A former boxer, he began our talk with a very unmayorlike jab at the appearance of his municipality. "These are ugly little towns, aren't they? You know why? Because in places like this you get economic activity based on exploiting a resource such as gas or coal, and towns begin merely as a temporary means of providing housing and services for the employees. And you get people who are either transferred here and have no intention of staying, or people who come up to make some money and then get out."

The highway spawned the first few shops and houses that sprang up near this former fur-trading post, but natural-gas drilling and processing nearby have swelled the town's population to 3,500. Wood-veneer mills have raised hopes for more permanent jobs, and the first forays into farming have begun, on land cleared by bulldozer.

Forestry and farming: Mayor Schuck hopes they indicate a growing stability in Fort Nelson. "Life here has something that's lacking in the big cities these days," he said. "And that's a sense of community."

North from Dawson Creek, the scenery undergoes a marked alteration. Rolling farmlands along the Peace River yield to solid forests and gorges cut by swift rivers. Finally, 350 miles north of Dawson Creek, I spotted snow-capped peaks. From the top of Steamboat Mountain I found a breathtaking view of the Rocky Mountains — a cavalcade of stolid, craggy sentinels marching off to the southwest, giant barbs lining both sides of a broad valley.

At Mile 357 I pulled over to fill a canteen from a sparkling spring. Water free of chemicals, air scented only with the fragrance of spruce and pine — these are among the benefits along the Alaska Highway. But for me the highway is its own best attraction, a gravel road in a world of pavement, a rough-cut passage through hundreds of miles of virgin terrain.

Sighting wild animals adds to the show. I once topped a hill and saw a cow moose and yearling calf browsing along the roadside. No bread-crumb beggars, they slipped into the woods when I braked. Porcupines waddled through ditches at evening. At dawn one clear day, I spotted a bald eagle, white head gleaming in the sun, soaring above a winding stream. Mountain sheep grazed on a nearby hill.

But the very remoteness that breeds such wild beauty has its drawbacks. Theo and Frauke Prystawik pumped me for world news as I wolfed homemade bean soup in front of a huge stone fireplace in the Highland Glen Lodge at Muncho Lake — to me, the most beautiful of the lakes along the highway. Forested mountains rose steeply above its crystal, shimmering water, and snowy peaks glistened in the background. "What's happening outside?" asked Theo. "There was a big summit conference in Europe about four months ago. Did anything come out of that?"

A bit of the Old World accompanied this German couple to Canada. Their log sleeping cabins are roomy, sturdy, and spotlessly clean. Every other day, Theo bakes bread in an open hearth oven that he built. A sauna nestles among the trees like a tiny alpine chalet. I met two guests who extolled the virtues of Theo's sauna. Dietrich Brand, 33-year-old lawyer from Yellowknife in Canada's Northwest Territories, and his wife, Katharine, agreed to introduce me to the classic sauna experience — broiling in the hut before cooling off in an icy lake.

We fired up the sauna stove with boughs of jack pine and entered when the little hut reached a temperature of 106° F. "The ice water will not be as bad as you think," said Dietrich reassuringly, as we sat, perspiring, on cedar benches. "The extremes seem to confuse the senses so you can't tell the difference between hot and cold."

Red as lobsters after 15 minutes, we emerged, jogged a hundred yards to Muncho Lake, and plunged in, scattering mushy ice out of the way. Immediately, a thousand needles pricked my skin. Dietrich, I decided, might be right about the body's confusion between hot and cold, but the combination still hurt. Admittedly, a quarter-hour after the two-minute dip, my skin tingled pleasantly and my spirits soared.

With the sauna, I had gone suddenly from a suffocatingly warm environment to a frigid one. Thirty-five miles north of the lodge, I did the opposite. It was a cloudy, chill day, dropping a cold rain, when I crossed the Liard River — a perfect day to sample the hot springs a mile past the bridge. I toe-tested the water before entering, for the temperatures can vary greatly. Finding it perfect, (Continued on page 36)

THE KLONDIKE GOLD RUSH

Gold nuggets tossed to the crowds from ships arriving at Seattle and San Francisco from Alaska sparked a frantic rush of prospectors to the region of Canada's Klondike River in late 1897. Stampeders by the tens of thousands—from all over the world, but mostly from the western United States—ferried up the long coast to Alaska and unloaded gear and food at Skagway or Dyea. Some spent weeks backpacking their ton of supplies up 16 formidable miles to the pass leading to Crater Lake, a source of the Yukon River. Others (below) hired packers and carts to haul their belongings. Many piled goods on wagons, travois, or sleds and drove teams of dogs, horses, oxen, or even goats. At The Scales camp below Chilkoot Pass (right), some gazed at the 30-degree incline of the 1,225-foot slope they must climb, sold out at a loss, and turned back. A few paid as much as ten cents a pound to have their gear hoisted on cables anchored to the rock atop the pass. But most people stood in line to plod, nose to heel, up the "Golden Stairs" cut into the snow of Chilkoot Pass. At the top, they cached their 50-pound packs and slid downhill for another load, often climbing the pass five times a day. On the Canada side, they paid duty to customs officials, descended a vast snowfield, pitched tents, and built boats while waiting for the Yukon River to thaw. With the melt, the hopeful prospectors sailed across Bennett Lake and soon reached the Yukon on their way to the Klondike River 600 miles northwest.

Braced against a driving autumn rain, a hiker stands at the crest of Chilkoot Pass. At his feet projects a support for an aerial cable lift, a remnant of the gold rush. The pass, a trail from Dyea, several buildings

in Skagway, and an interpretive center in Seattle form part of the new Klondike Gold Rush National Historical Park. When merged with a similar reserve in Canada, the park will continue north to Dawson.

Rock-torn water foams past boatloads of stampeders approaching the Whitehorse rapids on the Yukon River. A flotilla of more than 7,000 boats left Bennett Lake in late spring of 1898; some 150 crashed in this short stretch of white water. During the next month, the remaining boats landed at Dawson at the mouth of the Klondike River. Men raced to stake claims and sift the earth for nuggets. By 1905, the area had produced 100 million dollars worth of gold, but most prospectors dug out less than the cost of the trip. Some turned to grubbing for wages in mines owned by others (below). An exhausted prospector sprawled on a bed of boulders evokes the stampeders' claim that even some Yukon birds sang the lament: "I'm so tired."

31

*L*aced in autumn by golden trees, patterned tailings from played-out gold mines form sinuous ridges along the Klondike River near Dawson. In the early 1900's, dredges scooped into the earth, removed the gold, and left a new landscape of ridges and lakes. Rising costs stopped such operations by the 1960's. Today's inflated gold prices, however, have lured many placer miners back to the old mines and streams. Holding a whisk broom, Del Thachuk and two partners inspect a month's take of nuggets and dust from their claim in southern British Columbia. "If gold falls below $90 an ounce," Del says, "even the best miner on the best claim would have difficulty making a living."

Twisting arms of a massive glacier unite beneath Kaskawulsh Mountain in Kluane National

DEWITT JONES

Park — a wild tract of ice, rock, and meadow near the highway in the Yukon Territory.

I submerged in warm tranquillity. Pleasant as the immersion was on that chilly day, I could only imagine the luxury it must have been to the highway's mud-spattered builders whose bath water normally was drawn in a metal washtub.

Farther north, I crossed Contact Creek, meeting point in the autumn of 1942 of two Army units—one working north from Fort Nelson and the other coming south from Whitehorse in the Yukon Territory. On October 20, two other crews—one working south from Alaska and the other heading north from Whitehorse—met near Mile 1200. The union of the big cats in these two places marked the completion of the thread that tied Alaska to the "Outside." A ribbon-cutting ceremony on November 20 officially opened the route.

At a roadhouse south of Contact Creek I saw a reflection of how little the highway and the land it passes through have changed, even 35 years later. The dining room of the Fireside Inn overlooks the Liard River. Beyond the river, curving gently out of view, dark spruce forests stretch away to the horizon. Missing is the inevitable development—riverside housing, motels, hamburger stands—that would cluster around a more populated area.

All along the route, near lakes as beautiful as Tahoe, or mountains sculpted like the Tetons, the feeling of discovery persists. Teslin Lake enchanted me; about 80 miles long, it sparkled with diamondlike clarity at sunset. The free-running Liard River looks like the Missouri must have when Jedediah Smith saw it, winding through land unbroken by a plow.

At Mile 588.4 I entered the Yukon Territory, and for the next 40 miles crossed and recrossed its border with British Columbia nine times. The scenery, of course, ignored political boundaries: I drove a serpentine roadway that writhed through limitless trees and skirted pristine lakes. Watson Lake might have remained one of those quiet, little-known lakes had it not acquired a military airstrip in the late 1930's. Today the strip serves commercial airliners and charter planes transporting fishermen and hunters into the wild. The businesses and homes of Watson Lake, population about 1,000, are scattered along the highway for three miles, like swallows' nests clinging to a railroad bridge.

"This will always be Watson Lake to me," said Vic Johnson, at his home near a smaller settlement seven miles north of the highway. In 1938, Vic went to work at the military airport and watched a town grow out of the woods. "That's the old post office right over there," he said, pointing to a sagging, decaying building. "I like this old part of Watson Lake better than that thing they call a town along the highway."

Towns, as well as homes, may be where the heart is. To dozens of young Canadians, Vic's small spread will ever be a part of home. During the past 30 years, Vic and his wife, Catherine, have served as foster parents to 189 sick, mistreated, or abandoned children—besides rearing four of their own.

The Johnsons seem to have trouble casting anything aside—old cars, tired television sets, worn-out refrigerators, youngsters. All are found in the acreage around their shack. Amid the flotsam of their past scampered three small children who called the tall, bent, 75-year-old Dane "Daddy."

36

I followed Vic into his house to meet the mother of 189. "We kept 22 children one summer," said Mrs. Johnson with a smile. We talked as she ladled large helpings of spaghetti from a huge pot to the plates of foster children and visitors lined up at a long counter. "Some were youngsters the authorities had asked us to care for, and some just appeared at our doorstep. We had a group of teenagers and nine little ones in diapers. I had potty chairs lined up here in the kitchen because I couldn't be running to the bathroom with someone all the time."

Besides the Johnsons and their children, Watson Lake's biggest attraction is a bunch of signs. During the war, a homesick American soldier tacked up a placard announcing the distance to his town. Over the years, others have added their thoughts until now the signs stretch a hundred yards long and twenty feet high. I found greetings from all over the United States—Peoria, Illinois; Symco, Wisconsin; Albion, Maine; Moose Lake, Washington. Near the bottom I was happily surprised to find a sign left by a childhood acquaintance, Jerry Powell, of Wellman, Iowa.

FARTHER NORTH, IN TESLIN, I learned that an automobile had preceded the highway by more than a dozen years. In 1928, a barge carried the first car from Whitehorse to Teslin, a Tlingit Indian village on the eastern shore of Teslin Lake. The owner was George Johnston, a Tlingit trapper, who bought the Chevrolet after a bountiful year on the trapline; he built his own five-mile-long road to drive it on.

In the company of Sam Johnston, chief of the Teslin Tlingits and a nephew of George Johnston, I walked to the lakeshore to see the road. "For a small price, Uncle George would take you for a ride," Sam told me, as we followed the trail, now nearly overgrown with brush and saplings. "In winter, when the ice gets four feet thick, he could drive on the lake. It was hard to get tires out here then, so he would patch the ones he had with moose hide.

"When the Army was building the Alaska Highway, it merged with Uncle George's road a couple of miles up that way," he said, pointing to the north. "A bunch of soldiers got in jeeps and drove to Teslin. That was the most incredible sight people here had ever seen, those jeeps driving into town on Uncle George's road."

More than the quiet of Teslin was shattered by the growl of engines that day. The new highway brought a new way of life. "Alcoholism is killing the people here," Anglican clergyman Dan Sargeant told me over tea in his study. "Many have lost the meaning in their lives, with the change from a survival culture to a commercial one. They've lost their self-respect. These were once a proud people with depth, and a skill for survival under difficult conditions."

With those skills, George Johnston had wrested a living from the wilderness, and bought his showpiece car with the surplus. It was not the rigors of the trapline, however, that ended his life in 1973, when he was in his seventies. "He died of exposure one night after leaving a party," Chief Sam Johnston said quietly.

Near Marsh Lake, 70 miles past Teslin, bulldozers and earthmovers widened and filled the road for another stretch of pavement. "One of our problems here is swamp," highway project supervisor Gerry Cole shouted above the roar of heavy equipment.

Unstable ground has always been a problem. In the summer of 1942, muskeg sometimes nearly swallowed the Army's tractors and trucks. Bridging these bogs with corduroy roads—logs placed crossways in the muck—offered only a temporary solution. In the all-weather road that followed, the private construction firms placed a layer of rock over the muskeg, but mushy spots called "frost boils" still developed.

"Today we dig out the muskeg right down to a firm base, and then build up from there with granular matter," yelled Gerry over the din of a bulldozer. "We'd better get out of the way or we'll be part of it."

VIOLENCE IS NO STRANGER to life in the north. Whitehorse, the only Canadian municipality along the route large enough to be called a town when the highway was built, originated because of a violent stretch along the Yukon River. With the discovery of gold in the Yukon Territory just before the turn of the century, thousands of stampeders headed north to the rich fields along the Klondike River. Most of them climbed the snowbound Chilkoot and White passes near the coast, then floated down the Yukon from Bennett Lake, pausing below those rapids long enough for the town of Whitehorse to get its start.

"The stampeders had to brave Miles Canyon near Whitehorse," tall, bearded Keith Tryck told me. "There, some went around the dangerous rapids by tramway, reboarded their boats, and sailed on to Dawson. But many, like my grandfather, built a boat at Bennett Lake and rode it straight through the canyon."

In a canoe, Keith and I approached Miles Canyon, where in one week at the height of the Klondike Gold Rush the white waters and a series of rapids below the canyon claimed 150 boats. In 1972, re-creating the odyssey of his grandfather, Keith and three friends built a large log raft near Bennett Lake and traveled down the Yukon River 1,850 miles to the Bering Sea. Although the surging waters of Miles Canyon have been tamed by a dam, a collision with one of the narrow canyon walls still splintered part of their raft and nearly disabled it. "But we won't have any trouble with the canoe," said Keith.

So whisper-smooth was the voyage through Miles Canyon that we turned and paddled back out, a feat unthinkable three-quarters of a century ago. Survivors then were grateful to pause for a rest on the riverbank below the torrent. Around that haven, Whitehorse was born, perhaps as a place for stampeders to dry their socks. When the gold rush ended, Whitehorse survived as a transportation hub—the northern terminus of the White Pass & Yukon railway, and head of navigation for the river.

"Whitehorse was never really a boomtown," I was told by Dorothy Scott, whose father, W. L. Phelps, was the town's first attorney. "The men here worked for the railroad or on other salaried jobs, and the women were nurses and schoolteachers."

"It was a clean, neat little town," added her husband, John Scott, whose father also came with the wave of gold seekers. "There was a formal social life, and people often came to dinner parties in evening dress."

An island of humanity in a sea of wilderness, Whitehorse has more than doubled its population to about 14,000 in the past 15 years, an expansion that augurs continuing change for the vast areas around it. One hundred miles to the west, a section of wilderness more than half the size of Switzerland has been dedicated as a monument to nature.

Beyond the small community of Haines Junction loom the white-robed peaks of the St. Elias Mountains, a cluster of majestic heights as sacred in appearance as they are in name. They mark the outposts of Canada's Kluane National Park, where the emphasis is on wilderness preservation and minimal development. "The idea is to keep the area as natural as possible," explained park superintendent Sandy Rolfson as we flew in a helicopter over the 8,500-square-mile sanctuary. "We will probably create no visitor shelters and develop only trails, a few primitive campsites, and perhaps a road or two."

For the backpacker, that leaves mile after mile of untracked wilds imbued with a sense of space and freedom, filled with animals that roam unmolested by man. For the experienced mountain climber, it offers some of the most inaccessible and challenging terrain in the world—valleys perennially draped with glaciers and jagged summits where icy winds never rest.

"You will be seeing the land as the first settlers saw it when they came to this part of the world," said park naturalist Brent Liddle as I prepared for a solo hike into the Kluane lowlands. "There are a few mining roads, but that is the only modern activity in the park, and those roads are rapidly becoming overgrown. The park has some of the highest concentrations of wildlife in the Yukon, especially grizzly bear and Dall sheep."

Kluane spread a fascinating display of nature before me as I hiked to Sugden Creek, some 14 miles into the park's wilderness. In a valley between high ridges, I spotted several groups of Dall sheep, which are protected here from hunters. Oblivious to my field-glass intrusion, they grazed dizzying pastures, seeming tiny and vulnerable against the rock steeps, but nimble and sure in their steps. It was lambing season, but I failed to spot any little ones. Two rams butted heads in ritualistic battle—a sight viewed by few hikers, Brent Liddle told me later.

They stood quietly side by side, but facing in opposite directions. Suddenly, each walked about ten paces, wheeled, reared up, and charged. A sickening thud of horn against horn reached me nearly two seconds later. For long moments after the blow, they stood facing each other, heads tilted slightly, as though contemplating powerful headaches. The contest ended after several such charges when one reared halfheartedly, then dropped his head to graze.

At the edge of the Kaskawulsh River, an otter swam almost to my feet, snuffling loudly to catch my scent. Later, arising from a rest, I startled a bull moose that had wandered from among nearby trees. It stared at me for a second, then quickly trotted for cover.

That evening, camped on a high slope, I viewed a three-mile-wide panorama with binoculars, and finally saw what I had hoped to see—at the distance that I preferred to see it. Across the Kaskawulsh, on a steeply rising slope, was a grizzly bear feeding on a plant called wild sweet pea.

39

Unknown to the shaggy giant, three Dall sheep were attempting to pass its feeding ground on their way to higher pasture. For an hour I watched as the sheep, downwind from the bear, awaited their chance, moving to cover when the predator wandered near, reappearing when it drifted away. Finally, the bear ambled downslope. The sheep, screened by a slender stand of poplars, scurried up the hill, like the three billy goats gruff eluding the troll at the bridge.

Fear of grizzlies has curtailed visits to the park, naturalist Brent Liddle told me. "But if a grizzly knows you are coming, I would say that in virtually every case it will get out of the way. The worst thing you can do is surprise one, because at a range of 50 feet or less it feels threatened and may charge." I made sure that any bears knew exactly where I was at all times. I sang and whistled my way through thickets, and scanned the area ahead when walking in meadows. I saw tracks, many of them fresh, that a dinner plate would not hide, but encountered no bears closer than the one I had spied on with my binoculars.

Like many other travelers on the Alaska Highway, I saw Dall sheep where the road skirts the bottom of Sheep Mountain at the edge of Kluane Lake. There, the delicate, snow-white creatures can be seen grazing and frolicking among the cliffs.

The character of the Alaska Highway changes dramatically at Mile 1221.3 — the international boundary. Much of the adventure is then over, for ahead stretches a gray ribbon of asphalt with paved shoulders and yellow dividing lines.

Beyond the Alaska border, at Tetlin Junction, I stopped at Forty Mile Roadhouse, where Mabel Scoby presided over the gallons of coffee and the chicken-fried steaks. This roadhouse is not a tourist target, but anyone is welcome who doesn't mind sharing a long table with strangers and sitting on a spruce bench made by Ray Scoby 30 years ago. When I entered, Mabel was standing behind the counter, her hair a white froth around her face. "Don't get in a word war with Mabel," a trucker had warned me. "She'll leave you feeling lower than a snake's belly."

Mabel laughed at the mention of her reputation. "Oh, I've gotten mad a couple of times. One man came in and wanted his eggs a certain way. I fixed them like he said, but he wanted them done again. When I brought them to him the second time I said, 'Mister, you eat those eggs or you'll be wearing them out the front door.'"

Truckers provided most of Mabel's business. Their big rigs were parked at all angles outside the door, often hiding the well-weathered log restaurant. "I don't know them all, but I know most of them," said Mabel.

"They know you though, Mabel," a voice called above the clatter of forks. "I heard about you way down in Idaho."

The drivers may curse the curves and dust, but they retain a certain pride in their route. Sharing a table with Tom Ely and Lee Adams, I told them of a rookie Alaska Highway driver I had encountered in Fort Nelson who had called the road "a disgrace, a poor excuse of a highway." Lee Adams flared at the words. "He won't last long in this country with that kind of attitude! We can do without his type!"

"The road can be dangerous, though," conceded Tom Ely.

Snowmelt mirrors a service station in Tok, Alaska. Roadhouses offering food, beds, and gas border the route about every 50 miles. For its 300 miles in Alaska, the highway becomes a smooth, blacktopped thoroughfare.

Lee added: "The worst riding you can get is on snow when the temperature warms up and it gets so slick that you put chains on everything but the steering wheel."

"You get varying temperatures going up and down the hills," explained Tom. "Most of us keep a thermometer on the rearview mirror outside our cabs, to watch for warm spots."

Before trucks, dogsleds were the main conveyance in much of Alaska. At Tok, 12 miles north of Forty Mile Roadhouse, I discovered that sled dogs still hold an important position. "The pendulum is swinging the other way on use of dogs in these parts," said Roger Reitano, who raises and races Siberian Huskies and makes the wooden sleds they pull. "The Natives who switched to snowmobiles a few years ago are discovering that the machines are less dependable. If one breaks down 40 miles from home, you have to walk back. With a dog team, you can be half frozen and crawl into a sled, cover up with blankets, and tell your leader to go home and he'll do it. A machine won't."

Tok has attracted sled-dog breeders because of the extreme cold, Roger explained as we walked toward his kennels. "The snow comes early, it's dry, and it packs hard," said the rangy musher, who stays wiry by running after his teams to keep them in training for big-money races in Anchorage, Fairbanks, and Tok. "Dog mushing is the official sport in Alaska."

Not a bark greeted us as we reached the wire fence surrounding the kennel. "Now watch what happens when I walk through the gate," said Roger. He entered the enclosure and immediately 46 canine voices were raised in a whining, yipping chorus, while bodies pulled against chains. He patted a dog here, talked to one there, hugged a favorite; when he left, quiet returned. "They run hard because they are highly bred and want to please me," he said with satisfaction. "Some sled dogs are whipped in training. If one of my dogs isn't good enough to race, I'll put it to sleep before I'll sell it to a whip driver."

41

Although the Alaska Highway officially ends at Fairbanks, the Richardson Highway between there and Valdez was already in existence when the wartime route was built. Delta Junction, where the two highways meet, was a construction camp for the Alaska Highway. But today, it is oil talk, not highway talk, that quickens the pulse, for the pipeline from Prudhoe Bay to Valdez runs through here.

"Right now, I think we're in the same position that California was in when gold was discovered in 1848," said Delta Junction Mayor Bob Cramer in his Club Evergreen, a watering spot for pipeline workers. "We have the highway, and there's talk of a railroad going through to Watson Lake. You're going to see a lot more people coming up here."

Only those who welcome a challenge will stay, observed a longtime Alaskan, Knut Peterson, who lives in a tiny shack along the highway north of Tok. At 82, Knut has seen much of both change and challenge in the north, and is writing a book about his experiences, including being mauled by a grizzly. "There's kind of a stampede to the North Slope right now," he told me, "but those people don't have many plans for staying and helping the country. They just want to make money. For those who work hard and care about the land, there is still plenty of challenge."

Weather, terrain, economic activity, social development — maybe it's in the sharp bite of the clean air, or the immensity of an uncrowded land, but the challenges seem somehow more clear and focused in the north. I remember a chill October afternoon when the rocky, stairstepped slopes of a mountain rising just east of Whitehorse lured me to stretch my legs for a few idle hours.

It was late afternoon, and I had intended to mount just two or three levels of the steeply tiered slope and return before dark. But upon topping each rise, I wondered what lay on the next level, so I scaled one, and then another, and then another, until Whitehorse lay like a toy village far below, and the final rampart of stone seemed to loom above.

The sun was low, but I felt something unfinished, so I scaled a nine-foot rock wall and crossed a steep snowfield — only to find yet another bluff. The sun hovered just above the horizon, but I started up anyway. My breath whistled from the bellows in my chest, and with each step I was racked with pain in muscles and joints; I gasped aloud, perhaps to the mountain itself, "Please, no more summits."

I was learning something about the challenge of the north of which Knut Peterson had spoken. But with that challenge comes reward, I discovered, when I gained the top of the mountain. I marveled at the panorama of lakes, rivers, and peaks that spread before me, emblazoned by the sun that flickered and sank behind a saw-toothed ridge.

Still panting, I turned and quickly retraced my steps before my route was lost in the dark. Someday I plan to go back and enjoy the view.

Ears perked, a red fox — predator of small rodents — listens to woodland noises near the photographer's home in Whitehorse, capital of the Yukon Territory. Motorists driving the Alaska Highway may encounter a wide range of wilderness creatures; porcupines, Dall sheep, grizzly bears, otters, eagles, and moose all add to the adventure of following this winding link to the north.

WAYNE TOWRISS

RUNNELS OF FOG crawled down a precipitous cliff, probing the rock like ghostly fingers. Huddled against the October cold, I drifted in a rowboat on Turner Lake—a fiordlike slash of fresh water deep in the wilderness of a glacier-carved valley. Rain from pewter clouds marched across the lake toward me, finally coalescing with the drenching spray of a waterfall tumbling down the cliffside nearby.

On the far shore rose the wispy smoke of a wood fire I had kindled in the cabin where I was staying. Longing for its warmth, I began rowing into a quickening headwind that drove the rain like needles.

That evening, finally dry, I lay in my sleeping bag before the fire and reflected that I had sampled part of the lure—and the reality—of Alaska: its harshness.

"Ja, it's a tough country and it takes tough people to live here—you learn quick whether you can take it or not," Tiger Olson told me a couple of days later. A prospector and trapper "somewhere in my eighties," Tiger lives a solitary life in a small, neat cabin at Taku Harbor, 20 miles southeast of Juneau.

He scratched the grizzled stubble on his chin and added with a broadening grin, "Of course, we had to be a lot tougher when I came to Alaska 65 years ago. Two friends and I headed north out of Seattle in a rowboat bound for Juneau. There had to be three of us. We needed one man to row, one to bail, and one to holler for help!"

Today, sleek ferries of the Alaska Marine Highway System churn through the same island-dotted waters from Seattle to Skagway, serving as the main transportation link in Southeastern Alaska. Riding these ferries, I had an unparalleled view of the terrain and wildlife of the Southeast. In an almost endless display, whales sound, porpoises frolic, and eagles soar. Mountain ranges draped with Sitka spruce, western hemlock, and yellow cedar jut thousands of feet above the salt water; huge grumbling glaciers course back to the sea, where they calve icebergs of monumental proportions and bizarre shapes.

The geography captivated me; to learn of its origins, I sought out John Knorr, a tall, sandy-haired naturalist with the U. S. Forest Service. "Almost everything in this part of Alaska was formed by glaciation," he said. "Some 10,000 years ago a massive ice sheet more than a mile thick blanketed all of Southeast. As it advanced, it cut and gouged the land, forming the distinctive islands and canals, fiords and inlets that we see today. Right now we're in the midst of a 'little ice age' which began about 4,000

Abstract faces peer from a handwoven Chilkat robe made of mountain-goat wool and cedar bark. Chiefs and leaders of high social rank of the Tlingit Indian nation—the predominant Native group in Southeastern Alaska—wore such robes in ceremonial dances. This blanket personifies Herring Rock, a sacred natural formation near a herring-spawning area in Sitka.

the Southeast

By William R. Gray

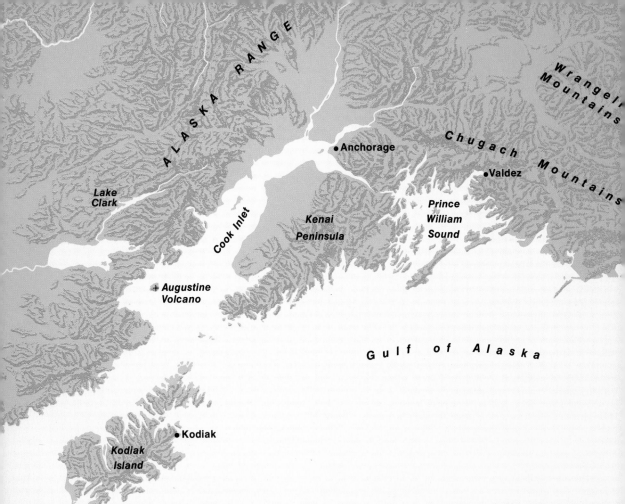

ALASKA RANGE

Wrangell Mountains

Chugach Mountains

•Anchorage

•Valdez

Lake Clark

Cook Inlet

Kenai Peninsula

Prince William Sound

+ Augustine Volcano

Gulf of Alaska

•Kodiak

Kodiak Island

SOUTHEASTERN ALASKA

"A picture of icy wildness unspeakably pure and sublime," wrote naturalist John Muir of the glacier-formed rawness of Southeastern Alaska. *"But out of all the cold darkness and glacial crushing and grinding,"* he recorded, *"comes this warm, abounding beauty and life...."* Today, forests of spruce and hemlock and meadows decked with wild flowers border the glaciers and jutting peaks of the region. Malaspina Glacier, North America's largest, scours a path as wide as 50 miles from the heights of the St. Elias Mountains. A warm ocean current brings a temperate climate to the Southeast, but fog and rain often shroud the lush, rain-forested islands and the snowy peaks of the Coast Mountains. In Southeast, Tlingit and Haida Indians have rekindled their cultural heritage, preserving crafts and traditions in communities like Klawock and Sitka.

ALASKA

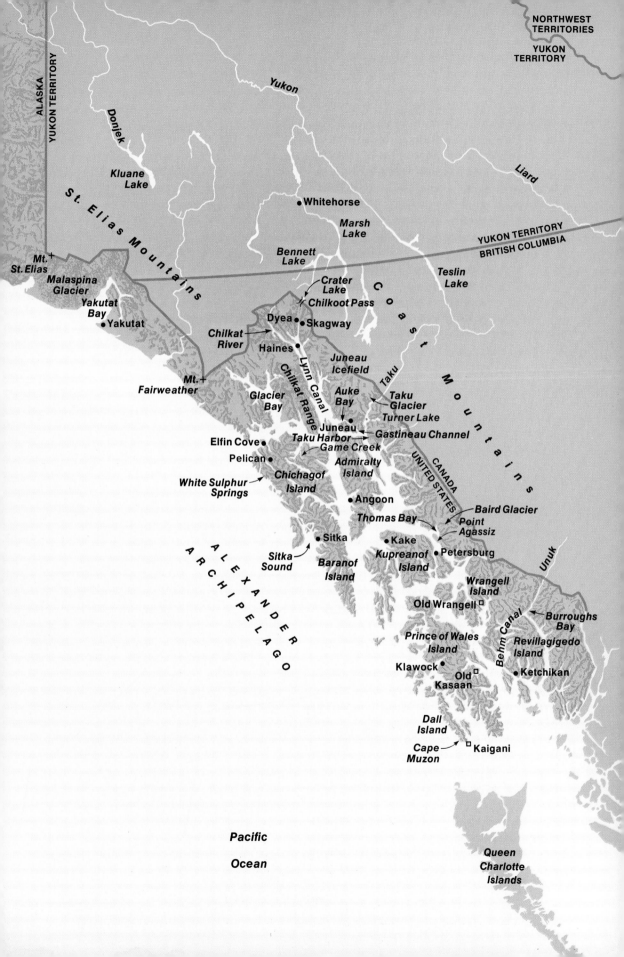

NORTHWEST
TERRITORIES

YUKON
TERRITORY

ALASKA

YUKON TERRITORY

Donjek

Kluane
Lake

St. Elias Mountains

Yukon

• Whitehorse

Marsh
Lake

Bennett
Lake

Liard

Teslin
Lake

YUKON TERRITORY
BRITISH COLUMBIA

Mt.
St. Elias

Malaspina
Glacier

Yakutat
Bay

• Yakutat

Coast Mountains

Crater
Lake

Chilkoot Pass

Dyea • Skagway

Chilkat
River

Haines

Juneau
Icefield

Taku

Mt.
Fairweather

Glacier
Bay

Chilkat Range

Lynn Canal

Auke
Bay

Taku
Glacier

Turner Lake

Juneau

Taku Harbor

Game Creek

Gastineau Channel

Elfin Cove

Pelican

White Sulphur
Springs

Chichagof
Island

Admiralty
Island

UNITED STATES

CANADA

• Angoon

Baird Glacier

Thomas Bay

Point
Agassiz

Sitka

Sitka
Sound

Baranof
Island

• Kake

Kupreanof
Island

• Petersburg

A L E X A N D E R

Wrangell
Island

Old Wrangell □

Unuk

Burroughs
Bay

A R C H I P E L A G O

Prince of Wales
Island

Revillagigedo
Island

Behm Canal

Klawock •

Old □
Kasaan

• Ketchikan

Dall
Island

Cape
Muzon

□ Kaigani

Pacific

Ocean

Queen
Charlotte
Islands

years ago. That's when the Juneau Icefield and the current glaciers began to be created.

"The Juneau Icefield and its glaciers," John continued, "form an expanse of ice nearly 2,000 square miles in extent. Thirty-five glaciers plow down from an elevation of about 5,000 feet, and some don't stop until they reach salt water; we call these tidewater glaciers."

On a sunny October afternoon—a rarity in rainy Southeast—I flew in a chartered plane over the Juneau Icefield. It sparkled in the sunlight, a sprawling plateau of dazzling white marked by the black peaks of nunataks—sharp-edged mountains poking above the ice. Our plane swooped low over several of the glaciers, which spread from the icefield like giant, sinuous tentacles.

I was particularly drawn to Taku Glacier; born in the fresh snows of the icefield, it emerged as a bare river of ice, wound through steep-walled canyons, and finally plunged into the swirling gray waters of Taku Inlet. On its broad back, contorted by pressure and the shape of the land it passes over, crevasses yawned widely, revealing a shrill, deep blue.

Seeing the power of that glacier and the ways it has shaped the land, I could easily envision how, during the Ice Age, ice sheets a hundred times that thick could have bullied the land into its current dramatic form. Glaciers, in fact, are so fundamental to this part of Alaska that one of the most spectacular areas of glaciation has been made a federal reserve. Glacier Bay National Monument is a breathtaking arena of ice, rock, and water that crests at more than 15,000 feet atop Mount Fairweather. Ice covers much of the monument, and 16 tidewater glaciers end in salt water.

The rugged terrain of Southeastern Alaska harbors an extensive range of wildlife: land mammals such as bears, moose, and wolves; sea mammals such as whales, seals, and sea lions; and birds and fishes beyond count. Once, standing near a tidal flat, I looked up and watched a pair of white mountain goats grazing along the side of a steep cliff; then, simply by swiveling my head, I saw a pod of 20 porpoises leaping and splashing offshore. Hundreds of miles would separate these species elsewhere in the nation.

I flew over the White Sisters—small nubs of rock in the Gulf of Alaska off Chichagof Island—and found a rookery of sea lions. Three hundred of these lumbering mammals sunned on the rocks, and more dotted the sea. As we flew over, a few of the creatures heaved their ponderous bulks into the water; others crawled out of the crashing surf and shouldered space among their fellows.

On a tranquil Sunday afternoon, I watched wildlife from the back deck of Alice Cook's house on Auke Bay, just north of Juneau. Alice is an environmental educator with the Forest Service; a joyous woman with a broad smile and flowing brown hair, she would teach me much about Alaska's plants and animals. A pod of five humpback whales swam in Auke Bay, surfacing every few minutes to breathe in long gasps that sounded like hollow booming within a cave. Usually, their black shiny backs broke the surface in flowing arcs; but once, for no apparent reason, two of them hurtled skyward in a crash of foam, arched sideways in the air, and thundered back into the water with a towering splash.

Elsewhere in the bay, sea lions swam and ducks floated. Occasionally, a seal poked up its head, periscopelike, to survey its domain. Overhead coasted what to me is the most majestic of Alaska's creatures — the bald eagle. This bird has found a haven along the isolated, treelined coast of the Southeast. "As many as fifteen thousand eagles thrive in this area," Fred Robards, eagle management specialist with Alaska's Fish and Wildlife Service, told me in his Juneau office, "and the population is now fairly stable." A tall, graying man with sharp blue eyes, Fred added, "There's nothing like watching an eagle perched high in the branches of a tree suddenly take flight, dive toward the water, and emerge with a fish clutched in its talons. It's a spectacular display of natural ability."

I learned from Fred that bald eagles in Alaska often attain a wingspan of more than seven feet, and that they can live as long as 50 years. They nest in tall trees near the shoreline — a major concentration exists on untamed Admiralty Island. Mated eagles hatch two young in late May, and the parents care for them until they begin flying in August and can fish for themselves.

"The eagle population is very dependent on coastline trees," Fred said, "and timbering operations have threatened their habitat. We've finally negotiated an agreement that will protect a coastal strip of woodland wherever lumbering takes place. This should help ensure the stability of the bald eagle population."

Curious, I asked Fred what he most admired about bald eagles. "It's their tremendous capability. They are fantastically strong — their two-inch talons are frighteningly powerful and they have beaks designed for tearing flesh. They're quick and have extremely acute eyesight — an eagle can see a small fish up to a mile offshore."

Following Fred's advice, I journeyed up the Chilkat River about 20 miles northwest of Haines to see a gathering of these amazing birds. In winter, groundwater seepage keeps a three-mile section of the Chilkat thawed, and as many as 2,000 eagles fly to the area to feed on salmon carcasses left from spawning. Although it was only mid-October, and the first traces of snow were just beginning to deck the towering Chilkat Range, I still saw about 50 eagles at one time. Some stalked the riverbank; others perched in trees — all awaited the movement of fish in the water. For an afternoon, I studied these birds and their motions. Seeing the snow-white plumage of an eagle's head and the silvery-yellow glint in its eye, I could easily understand why Tlingit Indians chose this noble bird as one of their major clan emblems.

THE TLINGITS — and their neighbors to the south, the Haidas — migrated to the tidal areas of Southeastern Alaska thousands of years ago. They slowly established a seminomadic life based on fishing, hunting, and gathering wild plants. "Our ancestors developed an intricate culture and a unique civilization," Ellen Lang, superintendent of the Sitka National Historical Park, told me. A Tlingit Indian born in Sitka, Ellen is a slim woman with black hair touched by gray. She speaks with a quiet dignity.

"The Indian people of this region lived in a relationship with nature that was based upon profound respect and fear. They understood the universal power of nature and strived to live in harmony with it. Their closeness to the land and their love for it produced an extremely successful way of life.

"They were a seasonal people who lived in family clan houses, each big enough for 50 to 60 people. Several such clan houses would form a village. The first sign of spring was always the coming of the herring to spawn. This was a time of joy and liveliness, for it signaled the end of a long winter. Then came halibut and salmon in the summer and fall. Autumn was a busy time for preparing food for the winter—fish and meat would be dried, smoked, and cooked in various ways.

"The winters were the time for art, dances, song, and recalling history. The people made clothing and ceremonial costumes, fashioned canoes from logs, wove baskets from spruce roots, and carved useful and ceremonial objects from wood. Each clan had a series of emblems which identified it, and these symbols—representing various animals—were used to decorate the art. My jewelry, for instance, displays my clan emblems." She showed me graceful silver bracelets with designs of a raven and a frog.

To me, Tlingit art is unique, with flowing lines, stylized portrayals of Alaskan creatures, and subtle shadings of yellow, red, blue, and black. Ellen explained that Tlingit art is experiencing a renaissance. "Today, because of many forces, there is renewed pride in being a Native Alaskan, and that pride is reflected in such ways as increased interest in art." Ellen took me on a tour of the Indian Cultural Center at the National Historical Park, where Tlingit and Haida craftsmen work in wool, wood, and silver to create art ranging from totem poles to Chilkat robes—beautiful ceremonial garb.

"These people not only produce excellent Native art," Ellen said, "but they also give visitors a taste of our culture. Most importantly, though, they teach the children the foundations of the art and what that art has meant to our people. The traditions are continuing."

Several Native communities—Angoon, Kake, and Klawock among them—still cling to the traditional ways, I discovered. But the most haunting echoes from the past that I found were in long-deserted villages. At Cape Muzon, on Dall Island, I poked through the overgrown remains of Kaigani, a Haida settlement unlived in for more than half a century. Green growth had reclaimed the town, softening the work of man. Except for a few squared-off hand-hewn timbers that served as cornerposts for houses, it was hard to distinguish the town area from the surrounding forest.

An eerie silence pervaded Cape Muzon, a silence broken only by the murmur of the tide and the soft squishing of my boots in the damp soil. I felt in some way that I was violating a shrine. That feeling skyrocketed when, crawling over a fallen log, I confronted a primally frightening sight: the hollow, empty eyes of a human skull. An involuntary shiver crept up my spine and only slowly subsided. I stared at the stark bone, colored light green by splotches of moss, and wondered how it came to be in the log. After a moment, I quietly left.

On Wrangell Island, I found another reflection of the past. Stretching from shore into the gray waters of Zimovia Strait were more than 50 parallel rock walls 20 to 30 feet apart and three feet high. Each had been pains-takingly piled a rock at a time. These long-abandoned structures, I learned, served the village of Old Wrangell as protected berths for large seagoing canoes. Hollowed from long cedar logs, such canoes were used for fishing, transportation, and war.

Cedar logs served another purpose for the Tlingits — as totem poles. Carved with a series of figures, the poles were erected in villages to tell a story, to commemorate a special event, or to identify the owner by his clan emblems. By the late 1930's, most existing totem poles had been removed to protected totem parks near Ketchikan or in Klawock. The only pole I found standing where it had been originally placed showed the effects of time — but it still stood proudly, looming above the tideline at the deserted village of Old Kasaan on Prince of Wales Island. Leaning, gray with age, and charred by fire, the pole still commanded a dignity and evoked the artistic essence of another era. Near the top of the totem, a couple of hemlock seedlings grew, apparently drawing nourishment from the weathered pole. I reflected on what Ellen Lang had told me of the resurgence of Native art. In that totem pole sprouting a second generation of life, I saw a symbol of the new flourishing of the Tlingits' interest in their heritage.

THE HERITAGE OF SOUTHEASTERN ALASKA stems from many sources. In the late 1700's Siberian hunters of sea-otter fur sailed in flimsy craft across the Gulf of Alaska, finally reaching the Alexander Archipelago. In 1804, after two major battles with the Tlingits, a permanent Russian community was established at Sitka; it was called New Archangel. Governor Aleksandr Baranov — a capable administrator and tough disciplinarian — moved there, and, within a few years, the town became the capital of Russian America. "It grew into the biggest merchant and trading center on our Pacific Coast," said Jim Davis of Sitka, who received his doctorate in the Russian history of Alaska.

On a blustery afternoon, Jim and I walked through Sitka, and he pointed out remnants of the Russian culture. The most dramatic is the Cathedral of St. Michael, the Russian Orthodox church in the town center, which was rebuilt after catching fire in 1966. "New Archangel was a thriving community," Jim said, "and from here Baranov commanded a far-flung empire based on sea-otter fur. The fur trade was augmented by a sawmill, furniture factory, dockyard, foundry, and two breweries. In fact, the first steamship built on the West Coast was made here."

Our stroll ended high atop Castle Hill, where Baranov made his home. I could see waves from the open ocean as they marched into Sitka Sound and broke on outlying islands. It was on a similar October day in 1867 that the Russian colors were struck for the last time on Castle Hill. U. S. servicemen then raised the Stars and Stripes, and the United States assumed control of Alaska, which had been purchased from the Russians earlier that year.

The flavor of another European country pervades Petersburg, a fishing town on Mitkof Island. Peter Buschmann, a Norwegian, settled there around the turn of the century, and many of his countrymen followed. Their influence is still strong. An annual (Continued on page 68)

51

Norwegians in Alaska celebrate their heritage in Petersburg during an annual festival honoring their old country's Constitution Day—May 17, 1814. Descendants of Nordic fishermen who settled here dance the schottische (right) before a group of youngsters (above) in traditional dress. While many people rushed to Alaska for gold, these early Norwegian immigrants sought their fortune in fishing; Peter Buschmann, from whom the town takes its name, selected the present site in 1897, and built a salmon cannery. Today, this thriving town of some 2,500 people still bases its economy firmly on the sea. These Alaskans call their town "Little Norway," because the fiords and mountains of the Southeast remind them of their homeland.

Baird Glacier and snow-touched peaks of the Coast Mountains dwarf the **Wesley**, a shrimp boat fishing Thomas Bay. Wielding a net (below), Bill Greinier, captain of the shrimp boat **Charles W.**, scoops shrimp onto a sorting table. Bill and his one-man crew trawl for as much as 2,500 pounds of shrimp in a 14-hour day. At the Alaskan Glacier Sea Food Company's processing plant in Petersburg, workers immediately cook and shell Bill's catch, and then can the shrimp for shipment. "Ours is the last hand-shelling operation in Alaska," says plant owner Dave Ohmer. The waters of Southeastern Alaska yielded some 55 million pounds of fish and shellfish in 1975.

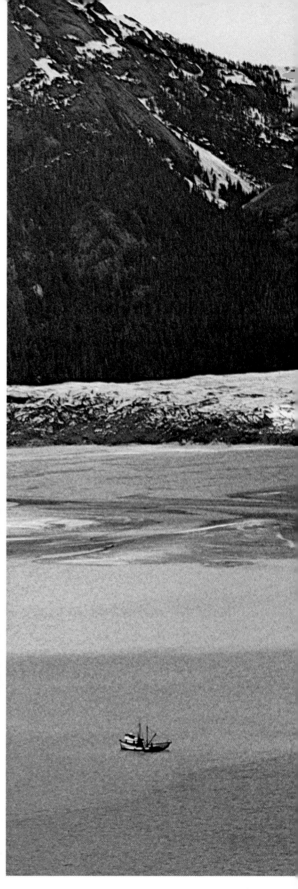

High tide fills Gastineau Channel, a narrow waterway near Juneau — Alaska's state capital.

Highrise structures mingle with turn-of-the-century frame houses in this city of 19,000 people.

O*n the floor of the State House of Representatives in Juneau, bearded majority leader Mike Miller gathers support for an impending vote during the 1976 session. "When the legislature convenes each winter," says a Juneau resident, "it's one of the most hectic and most enjoyable times of the year." The legislators, taking a break from the business of lawmaking, play softball against a team of townspeople on a rainy May afternoon. Representatives (left) cheer as a batter (below) eyes a pitch. Designated as the capital in 1900, Juneau may lose its status as the seat of government. In 1974, Alaskans voted to move the capital closer to Fairbanks and Anchorage—the state's main population centers. Isolated by weather and distance from most of the state, Juneau may become a virtual ghost town since the government employs about half of the work force. "This has got to be the ultimate in the throwaway society," says Mike Miller, who estimates that the move will cost a total of 2.6 billion dollars. Miller says he would take the capital to the people by televising legislative and committee sessions—at a fraction of that cost.*

Gnarled branches of a fallen tree arch above a clammer digging into beach gravel on an island

near Ketchikan. Some 150 inches of annual precipitation produce lush rain forests in this region.

*S*awdust flying, logger Kenneth J. Ewald fells a decades-old conifer at a timbering site near Sitka. Looking as thick as a shag carpet from the air, forests of spruce, hemlock, and cedar blanket much of the mountainous terrain of Southeastern Alaska. The Tongass National Forest, largest in the United States, covers 16 million acres of the Southeast and contains most of Alaska's timber resources. Of the 408,000,000 board feet cut in this area in 1975, much became pulp at the large mills near Ketchikan and Sitka. "The timber industry has historically been the main user of this land," says K. J. Metcalf of the Tongass National Forest. "But times are changing. Today we also need to consider the recreational and wilderness values of the land."

*E*yes *fixed on the cue ball, Slim Jim Foster lines up a shot in Rose's Bar &
Grill, most popular gathering spot in the town of Pelican. "It's so quiet here,"
says Rose Perley, owner of the bar, "that the birds and squirrels are noisier
than the cars. Of course, Pelican only has three large motor vehicles—a
garbage truck, an oil truck, and a fire truck." Pelican (left), a boardwalk town,
clings to a steep, narrow strip of land and a limited way of life—fishing; but
still it flourishes. A town of 200 people, Pelican opened a new crab cannery in
1975, and hopes soon to have a dock for the Alaska Marine Highway System
ferries. At Elfin Cove, a small community of about 30 people some 20 miles
north of Pelican, a couple embraces (top, left) while waiting for a boat to
Pelican—in winter, the nearest center for shopping and entertainment. A
local wag tacked up the highway sign on the dock in carless Elfin Cove.*

*B*ald eagle spreads its wings among the snowy branches of a tree along the Chilkat River near Haines. As many as 2,000 bald eagles gather here to feed on salmon carcasses exposed by a short, unfrozen stretch of the Chilkat River. Above, highbush cranberries flecked with snow symbolize the wild beauty of Alaska for the author. "That momentary glance gave me an understanding of why Alaskans care so much for the land," explains Will Gray.

NATIONAL GEOGRAPHIC PHOTOGRAPHER STEVE RAYMER (RIGHT); WILLIAM R. GRAY, NATIONAL GEOGRAPHIC STAFF

Norwegian Festival shows old country costumes and dances, and many of the surnames in Petersburg reflect their Scandinavian heritage.

It was from a man of French descent, however, that I learned of one of Petersburg's main fishing enterprises — shrimp. One day long before dawn, I boarded the *Charles W.*, a ship skippered by Bill Greinier. Deckhand Greg Foxley cast off, and we were soon churning south in Wrangell Narrows. With daylight came my first clear view of Bill and the *Charles W.* A second-generation Petersburg shrimper, Bill is a burly man with a quick smile; his boat is a beam trawler, 55 feet long and stripped down for work.

Soon we reached the west shore of Woewodski Island. Bill explained the operation as he and Greg began work. "We drop the trawl about 10 to 25 fathoms deep, and then drag it along and see what we get." The trawl is a huge net suspended from a 50-foot-long wooden beam. It splashed into the murky waters of Duncan Canal, a winch line the only evidence of its existence. For half an hour, we cruised the shoreline of the island; then Bill and Greg began to haul up the net.

When it broke surface, it seemed alive with a dynamic, sparkling pink. Thousands of shrimp — nearly a quarter of a ton — thrashed in the sunlight. They varied in size from two to ten inches. The catch was dumped onto a sorting table, and Greg set to work as Bill steered the boat toward the next fishing area. I helped Greg sort, first cleaning out the fish and seaweed, then dividing the shrimp into different classes. As we worked, Greg said, "We've hauled up about everything — from pieces of a rusted car to a ten-foot squid."

After four trawls and a catch of more than 1,600 pounds, we headed back to Petersburg, where the shrimp would be cooked, shelled, and canned. After we docked, workers emptied the catch into huge vats of boiling water. In just a minute or two the shrimp were cooked, and they floated to the surface. One of the cooks flipped a ten-inch shrimp to me. I tossed it back and forth in my hands until it was cool enough for me to snap off the head, peel back the shell, and take a bite. I tasted the sweetest, tenderest, freshest meat I have ever had. And I have not since been able to eat shrimp — fresh, canned, or frozen, deep-fried, boiled, or sautéed — without being disappointed.

Along with fishing, the Southeast's major industry is wood products. Tongass National Forest, largest in the United States, covers almost all of Southeast — some 16 million acres of hemlock, spruce, and cedar. Most timbering is by clear-cutting — felling all growth within a specified area — and much of the timber is processed into pulp.

Ketchikan Pulp Company, which has a long-term contract with the Forest Service, is situated on Ward Cove northwest of Ketchikan. As I approached the cove, I saw hundreds of logs floating in the water and a huge mill that pumped steam and smoke from a tangle of stacks. In his office, I visited Don Finney, shirt-sleeved vice president of KPC. "Most of our logging is done on Prince of Wales Island," he told me, "although independent loggers are scattered throughout the area. After being cut, the logs are gathered into huge rafts and towed from the logging site to be processed here.

"Basically, the manufacture of pulp is very simple: breaking down the

Sitka, once the capital of Russian America, hugs the stormy west coast of Baranof Island. Russian hunters of sea-otter fur settled here around 1800.

lignin—the material which bonds the wood together—and then purifying and baling the remaining fiber. First, the logs are barked and then chipped into small bits. Through cooking, washing, bleaching, and drying, the pulp is derived from the chips. The residue is formed into sheets, then baled and shipped. The companies that buy our pulp make it into cellophane or rayon fiber for clothing or drapes."

After I toured the mill—a technological wonder that quickly reduces trees to a material the consistency of a desk blotter—I pondered what I had learned. I was saddened to think that majestic, centuries-old trees were clear-cut from virgin forests simply to make throwaway cellophane wrappers. I wondered if there were other uses for these vast forest reserves in Southeastern Alaska.

Apparently others have wondered that, too, including officials of the Tongass National Forest. I talked with K. J. Metcalf, tall, mustached chairman of the new Tongass Land Management Planning Team. "For years, our primary concern was timber, and we were responsive to the timber industry. Oh, we developed campgrounds and recreation areas, but our main thrust was in timber. Today, the public is telling us different things, and we're reacting. We're taking a new overall look at our whole forest to develop a balanced land-use plan.

"We recognize, of course, the need to continue the wood-products industry. But we also realize that wilderness areas, campgrounds, and hiking trails are equally important. We also have to consider fish and wildlife and protect their habitats. We're working closely with the state government, Native groups, other federal agencies, and the public to determine

69

how much of each of these areas we need and where they ought to be located throughout the region.

"One of the problems we face is that much of the land in Southeastern Alaska is rock and ice; therefore the desirable areas for any activity are limited. For instance, a fertile valley with a good stream might be excellent for fish production, for timber, or for recreation — we have to decide which is the best use for that particular valley, and ensure that the other uses are met elsewhere. To decide these things, we need to have maximum public input — we're hoping for a wide range of support."

Such public reaction and citizen unity have helped the people of Yakutat — the northernmost community in Southeastern Alaska — thwart over-development. A small fishing village on the shore of Monti Bay, Yakutat was slated as the main staging and support area for offshore oil development in the Gulf of Alaska. "We decided that we weren't going to be bullied by the big oil companies," Yakutat mayor Larry Powell told me, "so we dug in our heels." Larry, a slim, articulate man of 36 with graying hair and a boyish smile, owns Yakutat's general store. He is married to a young Tlingit woman. "You have to understand that the Natives have lived in Yakutat for hundreds of years; during that time they have come to love and respect the land and what it produces. Those of us from other places came for pretty much the same reasons. We like the smallness of the town and the wildness of the land. And no one — Native or white — wants to see it changed dramatically.

"The oil companies had bought land right in the middle of town. That meant heavy industrial development — warehouses, docks, big equipment — near our homes and next to our school. That was too much for us. We on the city government sat down with leaders of the Native village corporation and decided what we wanted to protect and what we could sacrifice. We agreed that nothing should harm our major fishing or recreation areas, and that we wanted any buildup to be outside the town.

"The best way we found to approach all this," Larry continued, "was by using Yakutat's legal and regulatory powers. We formally petitioned the oil companies to slow development; we turned down requests for permits they needed; we brought suit against them to cancel the project until further environmental studies were completed. Our hope is that if we can control the pace of development, slow it down, minimize the impact, then perhaps it won't change our lives too drastically."

After talking with Larry, I explored Yakutat, a straggle of buildings surrounding a dock and an old cannery. Near the end of town, I discovered a small wild area — a marshy pool slowly filling as the tide flowed in. Ducks drifted on the water, and fish broke the surface every now and then. An abandoned fishing boat lay overturned on the shore, ramshackle and gray. The heavy overcast that had blanketed Yakutat all day suddenly lifted and, for the few seconds before it closed in again, the snow-clad ramparts of Mount St. Elias became visible far across Yakutat Bay. In that momentary tableau of mountain, sea, and boat, I glimpsed what Larry Powell is seeking to preserve. I felt gratified that Yakutat — and Alaska — has such men to work toward a reasoned future.

Like Larry, many people who come to Alaska and stay possess a certain strength—both of body and character—that allows them to survive, and even prosper, in the rugged land and harsh climate. I met such a person in Ketchikan. Terry Wills came to Alaska as a youngster with his homesteading parents, who settled on the broad Unuk River, northeast of Ketchikan. Terry grew up in the wilderness and learned its ways. At age 18, he began flying floatplanes for a small charter company in Ketchikan. Within a few years, he bought his own air-taxi service and built it into a profitable operation that grossed $700,000 a year. Now, just 33 years old, Terry has retired from the charter business. "I needed a change," said Terry, a sturdy, muscular man with a jet-black beard. "It wasn't fun anymore, and I never had enough time for myself."

Now, he does. He bought a home with five acres of land, a waterfall, and a large dock on Clover Passage, north of Ketchikan. There he berths the *Sea Bear,* his sleek 52-foot fishing boat, and his eight-seat floatplane. Terry was nailing carpeting into the galley of the *Sea Bear* when I arrived in May for a trip we had been planning for nearly eight months. He wanted to take me up the Unuk River to his parents' old homestead, which, after years of being deserted, he had recently purchased.

We cast off early the next day and motored up Behm Canal. Heavily timbered slopes slipped past on both sides. We stopped occasionally to fish and soon had enough red snapper for a feast. At our anchorage that night where the Unuk flows into Burroughs Bay, Terry and I set three crab pots—later we hauled up a dozen Dungeness crabs, each measuring more than a foot across.

Before dawn the next morning we were bucking the current of the Unuk in a small skiff. What had been spring in Ketchikan was still winter here: Snow held the ground, and a wind cold enough for January knifed through my clothes. After following several miles of ever-narrowing river, we reached a grassy flat and pulled to shore. A cabin of yellow cedar logs that Terry was just completing stood on the flat. It was surrounded by a scattering of saplings. "They're apple trees," Terry explained. "We always had them when I was a kid. The old trees are gone now, just like all of the old buildings."

As we walked around Terry's land, I could see the happiness in his eyes. With a satisfied smile, he said, "I've been told that Unuk means dream. There couldn't be a better name for this place."

THE HARDY PEOPLE OF ALASKA are not all men, of course. At Point Agassiz, a 25-minute boat ride from Petersburg, I visited Alice Farra, 45, and Ann Bailey, 59, who have established one of the most prosperous homesteads I have ever seen in Alaska.

The central focus of the spread is a large vegetable garden and greenhouse flanked by a root cellar, a two-story home, a work shed, a chicken house, and a rabbit hutch. "We built it all ourselves, all by hand," Alice said with pride. A tall, lean woman with swept-back iron-gray hair, Alice contrasts with the smaller, softer-looking Ann. "We cleared the land, and I built the house during one summer about five years ago—lived here ever since."

In her immaculate kitchen, Ann served me venison and vegetable soup followed by a huge fresh salad topped with tiny shrimp—everything either grown or gathered by the two of them. After lunch, Alice and Ann gave me a tour; the squawking of geese, hens, ducks, and dogs punctuated our conversation. I asked why they would want to homestead, to come to an isolated spot far from human habitation.

"We both just like doing things," Ann said, "and having the time and freedom to do the things that we want to do." Alice added, "There's always so much to do here—getting the garden and greenhouse started in the spring and tending it through the summer; hunting and trapping in the fall; repairing things during the winter. There's never been a moment of boredom.

"A lot of people said that Ann and I could never do any of this on our own. Well, I found out that three-quarters of what people thought I couldn't do, I could do easily, and that makes me feel good."

Alice paused, cocked her head, and said, "I can't think of anything better than what we have here. I'm staying until I can't go on any more. This is it for me, everything I've always wanted."

Far to the northwest, on Chichagof Island, I met settlers of a different sort. A religious group of 50 people was establishing a community on a marshy tidal flat along Game Creek. A floatplane landed me, and I slogged through half a mile of mud before I reached the temporary community center—a large Army surplus tent. There I talked with one of the elders, Sister Betty Banaszak, as she shelled fresh clams.

"We simply call ourselves Christians," she told me. "We are individuals who felt we had a call on our lives from the Lord; we are learning to live the simple life. We hope to have some permanent buildings up before winter and by next summer to be well established. Our goals are twofold: learning to live in relationship to wilderness and learning to find a deeper life in God."

It was nearing lunchtime, and the members of the community were gathering from their chores, the men from the sawmill where they were cutting timber to build the houses, and the women and children from tending the gardens and gathering food. I could tell by their faces that, should the community fail, it would not be for lack of industry or devotion. As I walked back to my plane, I could hear their voices raised in a hymn: "And whatsoever I do shall prosper."

During the flight to Pelican, a small village on Lisianski Inlet, I detoured to the rugged seacoast of Chichagof Island and landed near White Sulphur Springs. Sparkling water thermally heated to about 95° F. bubbles from the earth there, filling a rocky pool to a depth of four feet. I floated dreamily in the water, protected from the chill rain by a wooden lean-to. Just 30 yards away, breakers from the Gulf of Alaska boomed mightily on the rock-strewn coastline. Gazing at that display of wild, cold water, I felt even cozier in the massaging warmth, and I delayed the continuation of my flight for two hours to luxuriate in the spring.

At Pelican, the cold rain was in command, and I was soaked and chilled by the time I reached the home of Joe Paddock. To get there, I had walked from the floatplane dock along the main and only street in town—a mile-long boardwalk built on pilings. Most of the homes and stores in town front on this boardwalk and also perch on pilings. In the warmth of his dining room, Joe served me pickled black cod and coffee as he told me about Pelican. "The town grew up because of the good fishing around here. A cold-storage plant where fish are frozen and shipped to canneries was built back in the '30's, and the town gradually expanded. I was in charge of building the boardwalk; I'm proud to say it's still in good shape. Pelican's grown some in the last few years, but thank God it hasn't changed much."

Framed by a twisted tree, the Russian Orthodox Cathedral of St. Michael, rebuilt following a fire in 1966, dominates downtown Sitka. Russian influence here still shows in names and architecture.

Later in the afternoon, I accompanied Joe to Rose's Bar & Grill, the town's social center. I played pool, drank a beer, and found a spot to carve my initials in the already well-sculpted bar. During the afternoon there, I met most of the 200 citizens of Pelican, and I learned of a basketball game to be played that evening between the high-school team and a group of young workers from the cold-storage plant.

Because of the inclement weather in Alaska, basketball—not football or baseball—is the main sport, played both for relaxation and in competition between high schools; and it's a tough, fast-moving brand of basketball. That night, wearing a pair of borrowed sneakers, I joined the cold-storage team in Pelican's Quonset hut gymnasium. In a hotly contested match, our fish-packing five built up a ten-point lead, only to see it whittled away in the last couple of minutes. A 15-foot jump shot right at the buzzer gave the high schoolers a one-point win. I jokingly promised to get my revenge the next time I came to Pelican.

Like most towns in Southeastern Alaska, Pelican clings to a thin line of land between surf and mountain steep. The only difference between Pelican and the city of Juneau is that Juneau had a reason to grow up. Alaska's state capital and a metropolis of 19,000 people, Juneau still has boardwalks and floatplane docks—just like Pelican. But it also has freeways, plush hotels, and a skyline of multistory buildings. As in Pelican, though, the people still smile and say hello to you on the street.

I like Juneau; it has a comfortable mix of the historic and the modern, the rough and the refined. The old workings of the Alaska-Juneau Mine dominate the hills behind the city, in contrast to the glass-and-concrete state office buildings downtown. Murky bars with a rowdy clientele exist almost next door to fine restaurants catering to business people. On the waterfront, an old floatplane hangar and a wharf have been renovated into a shopping mall.

The business of politics in Alaska combines that same feel of the old and new. I visited the chambers of the House and Senate in the Alaska State Capitol Building and observed the familiar range of political maneuverings: impassioned speeches, interminable committee hearings, whispered deals made in the corridors. But many of the subjects being debated are brand-new—offshore oil, natural-gas pipelines, land use.

"Alaskans must make an incredible range of important decisions during the next five to ten years," Governor Jay S. Hammond told me in his office in the capitol. A robust man with a graying beard, Governor Hammond relaxed behind his cluttered desk, his tie loosened and his collar open. "I think all Alaskans realize that change is inevitable; it's how we deal with it that we must work out. I foresee continued population growth and continued pressure on social services; but I also foresee a continued emphasis by everyone on the quality of the environment and on the basic quality of life."

Most Alaskans I encountered during my travels—from loggers to conservationists—would agree with the Governor on the importance of preserving Alaska's land.

In Skagway, I again learned why. I had taken a state ferry up narrow Lynn Canal from Juneau, arriving on a bitter, windy afternoon. I quickly discovered that, in local tradition, Skagway is an Indian word meaning, appropriately, "home of the north wind." Next morning, I awoke to a strange silence—the wind had abated. I looked out the window of my hotel to discover the first snowfall of the year. Two inches of white already robed the ground, and a thick curtain of snow was still falling. I quickly dressed and began climbing a promontory east of town. Skagway, which has a distinct turn-of-the-century flavor in its architecture, looked even more Victorian when wrapped in snow.

As I walked, I listened to the flakes whispering through the trees and ticking lightly on the nylon of my parka. Underfoot, the new snow crunched softly; beneath it, brittle leaves of poplar and cottonwood crackled. The barren branches of trees were etched with white, and the rocks and stumps wore snowy caps.

In this realm of gray and white, I spotted but one flare of color: a clump of red highbush cranberries flecked with a few crystal snowflakes. In that single reflection of wilderness beauty, I saw why the Alaskans I had come to know so revere their land.

Tlingit Indian waves a placard that proclaims her heritage as she rides a parade float in the Alaska Day Festival in Sitka. The annual celebration commemorates the official transfer of Alaska from Russia to the United States on October 18, 1867; that ceremony took place on Castle Hill in Sitka, a town which for more than 30 years served as the capital of the new possession.

WILLIAM R. GRAY, NATIONAL GEOGRAPHIC STAFF

3/Urban Anchorage, the Wild

THE BEAR WAS A MONSTER EVEN FOR A KODIAK—ten feet tall and three-quarters of a ton. Burly and ferocious, the Kodiak is the world's largest bear and one of the most dangerous animals on earth. Old he-bears are especially unpredictable and notorious; they kill indiscriminately and even cannibalize cubs. This beast—a bad-tempered old boar—slept in its daybed on Afognak Island.

Unaware that he was entering the bear's domain, Al Burch, a deer hunter from nearby Kodiak Island, startled the animal from its sleep. The bear began nervously snapping its jaws. Burch knew that dread sound and a shock of recognition swept his body when he turned to look. The giant bear, only yards away, clambered to its feet, roaring down at him like an avalanche of savagery. It was so close that Burch could smell the bear's foul odor.

Then the bear charged forward on its hind legs, bellowing thunderously, raking away bushes and branches with its great claws. Burch forced himself to take his eyes off the bear for a second as he raised his rifle and sighted through the scope. He knew his only hope was a head shot. The image in the scope was blurred from being too close, but he saw the bear's eyes, magnified and glaring at him. The first shot exploded and tore into the bear's head, and it fell backward. A second one smashed into the neck, and the bear died.

I held the huge skull—as big as a watermelon—as Ben Ballenger of the Alaska Department of Fish and Game told me the story in his office on Kodiak Island. "A bear's skull gets thicker and harder with age," Ben explained. "This one is rock hard and two inches thick in places. Burch was lucky his first shot didn't ricochet off."

Later, on a flight around the 1.8-million-acre Kodiak National Wildlife Refuge—an area containing some 2,000 bears and covering most of the island—I got my first look at one of the big Kodiaks. It appeared suddenly, lumbering along a small beach at the edge of a dark spruce forest. We flew low, and it stood tall on its hind legs, swatting at us with huge paws. The brief encounter reminded me of a scene from *King Kong* and left me further impressed by the bear's indomitable nature.

Kodiak is a windswept island of mountain and forest where bears roam the land and king crabs rule the sea. This was the first stop in my travels through south central and southwest Alaska, regions of untamed land and hardy people where a step anywhere off the main road promises wilderness and rich adventure.

Brooding winter storm clouds loom above the village of Unalaska in the isolated Aleutian Islands, a far-flung archipelago stretching 1,100 miles toward Siberia. Russian hunters of sea-otter fur sailed to the Aleutians in the mid-1700's; they subjugated the native Aleuts and established the Russian Orthodox religion—still practiced in Unalaska's onion-domed church.

Aleutians

By Fred Kline

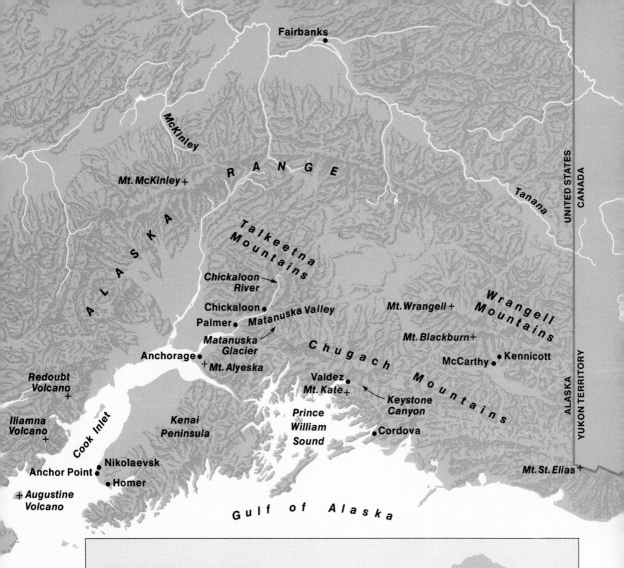

Fairbanks

McKinley

ALASKA RANGE

Mt. McKinley +

Talkeetna Mountains

Chickaloon River

Chickaloon

Palmer   Matanuska Valley

Matanuska Glacier

Anchorage   + Mt. Alyeska

Tanana

UNITED STATES
CANADA

Mt. Wrangell +

Wrangell Mountains

Mt. Blackburn +

McCarthy   Kennicott

Chugach Mountains

Valdez
Mt. Kate +

Keystone Canyon

ALASKA
YUKON TERRITORY

Redoubt Volcano +

Iliamna Volcano +

Cook Inlet

Kenai Peninsula

Prince William Sound

Cordova

+ Augustine Volcano

Anchor Point   Nikolaevsk
Homer

Mt. St. Elias +

Gulf of Alaska

Afognak Island

Kodiak

SOUTHERN ALASKA

Warmed by ocean currents and sheltered from frigid north winds by towering peaks, the south coast of Alaska supports most of the state's population. In contrast, the long, curving chain of the Aleutian Islands (below) has only tiny communities on a few of the larger islands. Geologically unstable, southern Alaska continues to record earthquakes and volcanic eruptions. Farms in the Matanuska Valley northeast of Anchorage yield vegetables, grains, and dairy products. Estuaries, inlets, and rivers provide rich spawning grounds for salmon and other marine creatures. Untapped oil and gas reserves in the Gulf of Alaska promise wealth—and environmental problems.

ALASKA

Unimak Island

Unalaska

Unalaska Island

Attu Island

Aleutian Islands

Atka Island

Amchitka Island

CONTINUATION OF ALEUTIANS FROM MAIN MAP

I had come to Kodiak at the height of the king-crab season, when most of the fishermen were out fighting storms along rocky coastlines for their prized catch. Most would stay out until the holds of their fishing boats were full—often weeks—and then race back to one of Kodiak's 13 processing plants to sell the crabs while they were still alive.

The king crab is a giant of the sea that can attain a leg spread of five feet and a weight of as much as 25 pounds. In the 1975-76 harvest, Kodiak's 200-boat fleet earned some 12 million dollars with a catch of 24 million pounds of king crab.

Kodiak crab fisherman Dave Kennedy invited me to accompany him on a one-day run to gather crab pots in the Gulf of Alaska. On a gray and rainy day, I boarded the *Dawn Treader,* a 75-foot vessel built to weather 100-knot gales, frequent icing, and high seas—routine conditions for Kodiak fishermen. I stood on deck enjoying the cold wind as we roller-coastered up and down the steep waves. Playful black and white Dall's porpoises raced close to the boat. Arctic terns and albatrosses hung like squawking mobiles in the sky. In the distance, whales blew quick fountains, almost invisible among the swelling waves.

Nearby, I spotted a line of pink buoys bobbing in the churning water. Attached to crab pots on the bottom, the buoys glowed like a string of party lights. Dave and his three-man crew soon turned to: retrieving the 600-pound pots with a hydraulic lift; tossing the spiny reddish king crabs into the hold; mending buoy lines; grabbing a smoke; stacking the pots as the hydraulic crane swung them to the stern; tying the pots down. There was hardly a break of more than a few seconds before it all started again. The men steadied themselves as Captain Kennedy maneuvered through the swells.

As my contribution to the work I carefully grabbed a wayward crab as it crawled off sideways across the deck. I approached it from the rear, gingerly picked it up by the shell, and quickly dropped it into the hold— a saltwater tank that keeps some 2,000 crabs alive. I avoided fist-size claws protruding from this eight-pound crab, an average commercial size. Its pincers could crush a finger.

Typical of Kodiak's fishermen, Dave Kennedy—a bearded six-footer— stands out as an uncommon man of many achievements. A former semipro football player, he holds a master's degree in fishing science and teaches at Kodiak Community College. He told me that he had decided to run for the city council and that the election was only a few days off.

"Kodiak needs a fisherman in city government," Dave said on the cruise home. "A representative from the town's leading industry ought to have a voice in policy making. The town is talking about taxing fishing boats on their raw sales. We're just going to have to fight it or we'll go broke." Later that week, Dave was elected.

At the Alaska Pacific Seafoods processing plant back in Kodiak, I sampled the tender white crab meat as it moved along a conveyor belt to be frozen. "Kodiak probably has the best fishing grounds in the world," said Dave, "but Russian and Japanese fleets have been grabbing the bulk of our fish and shellfish. If something isn't done, the fish will soon be gone, and with them our way of life."

What about the new 200-mile limit? "I'm cynical," said Dave. "I've seen what a political football fishing rights have been in the past." On April 13, 1976, a federal law was passed claiming exclusive jurisdiction and preferred harvesting rights for the United States in fishing grounds up to 200 miles off the nation's coastline. The law awaits testing until March 1977, when the zoning will go into effect.

FROM KODIAK I FLEW TO HOMER, where I began a 500-mile drive through stunning countryside: north up the Kenai Peninsula, then east through the Matanuska Valley, and finally south to Prince William Sound and Valdez. Within the first few miles, I was surrounded by sharp-crested mountains and deep forests of blue spruce.

Nine miles off the highway from Anchor Point I entered the village of Nikolaevsk, home of the Old Believers. A religious sect, the Old Believers adhere stringently to Russian Orthodox Christian ritual that dates to A.D. 988. Because they chose to ignore church reforms adopted during the mid-1600's, they were fiercely persecuted over the years in Russia. Finally, they fled from there in the 1920's and 1930's, settling for short periods in Manchuria, Hong Kong, Brazil, and Oregon. They found each of these places disagreeable for various reasons: politics, poor farmland, or, in the case of Oregon, proximity to the evils of a big city, Portland.

In 1967, seeking a more remote sanctuary than Oregon, the Old Believers bought land in an untamed tract of the Kenai Peninsula. Their goal, they declared, was to build a community where they could preserve the integrity of their faith and protect their children from modern temptations. Almost ten years after they first settled, I found a thriving community of 40 families—about 300 people.

Carved from the middle of a forest was a roughhewn frontier settlement. Some 40 frame cabins, expertly crafted from unfinished yellow spruce, lined both sides of the one main street in Nikolaevsk. The church, of similar construction, has two small onion-shaped domes; it is sacrosanct, and therefore closed to nonbelievers.

Some of the houses were painted in vivid colors: purple, yellow, pink, green. Bright colors that give "feelings of happiness" are a traditional part of the Old Believers' daily dress and a counterpoint to their religious orthodoxy. The men, who usually have beards, wear colorful hand-embroidered shirts called *rubashki*. The women always wear head scarves in public and have flower gardens of color decorating their long skirts, or *sarafany*.

Some of the men have become successful commercial fishermen, using the 34-foot fiberglass fishing boats that are built in the village. Others work in nearby Homer in canneries or at construction jobs.

While there are no television sets, radios, or musical instruments in Nikolaevsk, modern temptations of another sort exist. Cars, pickup trucks, and bulldozers go their clamorous ways. Children ride bicycles. A teenager on a motor scooter whizzes up the street, scattering a troop of geese. Most homes have washers and refrigerators, and all are heated by oil. Just five years ago most people burned wood.

Prohor Martushev and his son Kiril—both bearded and robust—greeted me from the foundation of a house they were helping a neighbor build. "We've just become American citizens," Kiril told me proudly. "Fifty-nine of us were sworn in just a few weeks ago. And today, we voted for the first time! Yes, Alaska is where we are going to stay."

I asked Kiril if the Old Believers had succeeded in their original goals of preserving their religion and protecting their children. "Our religion is still very strong," he answered. "Children usually go only to eight grades in school, and then they work and get married young. We have all changed in America, but the most important thing, our religion, has not. We are very happy here."

As I left Nikolaevsk to continue up the Kenai Peninsula, I looked across Cook Inlet; silhouetted on the horizon some 50 miles away were the imposing volcanoes Iliamna and Redoubt. Nearby, birches yellowing in autumn brightened the dark woods, but their leaves were falling, and a touch of winter was already in the air.

Most of the Kenai Peninsula is occupied by the Kenai National Moose Range, a 1.73-million-acre wilderness containing a controlled population of 9,000 giant Kenai moose. One of the most important wild game animals in the state, the moose is a valuable source of meat to Alaskans who live near its forestland habitat.

I prefer to hunt animals with binoculars. Armed with these "eagle eyes," I hiked into the moose range early one cold October morning and made camp after about five miles. The only wildlife I had seen on my hike were Canada jays, but many tracks dotted the light covering of snow: moose, weasels, hares, voles, and a single wolf.

At the edge of a nearby pond, I climbed a tree and waited. By sunset, three hours later, I had excitedly watched a large bull moose with great winglike horns drink from the sparkling water. As elated as I was with this sight, it was only a preliminary to what followed later.

At one in the morning, I awoke and walked outside my tent. There I saw an enthralling display of the aurora borealis—northern lights that explode with color as charged particles from the sun collide with earth's atmosphere. The ghostly lights veiled the stars and began to flicker and gleam, now here, now there. They swirled in red-fringed curtains of light, yellow and blue feathers of light, and green arcs of light. They crackled like distant cellophane as they changed and drifted in the celestial wind.

I like the game Eskimo children play with the northern lights. They whistle at them, trying to call them to earth. Then the children run and hide before the luminous spirits can grab them.

Farther north, George Mobley, photographer for this book, joined me for the continuing drive to Valdez. Along the way, we saw many patchwork homesteads, both large and small. Long an Alaskan tradition, homesteading, with its federal grant of 160 acres to anyone willing to try his luck, ended in 1974 amid the clamor of Native claims and land-use controversies. A famous group of homesteaders came to Alaska from the Lower Forty-Eight in 1935—during the Great Depression. They settled in the broad Matanuska Valley near Palmer, less than an hour's drive northeast of Anchorage.

These hardy pioneers were part of a federal program to settle and farm Alaska's difficult land. Due to the efforts of these homesteaders, the

Matanuska Valley has become Alaska's agricultural heartland, with many dairy farms and rich fields of grain, hay, and vegetables. Of the some 200 families who volunteered back in those Depression days, a third left within a year. Only a handful of the original settlers remain today.

In the midst of fertile fields, in the ranch-style house they built and added to over the years, I met one of those original couples—Joseph and Naomi Loyer. They are now retired from farming, but still maintain a small dairy. And of the 11 children they reared on the farm, nine still live in Alaska. George Mobley and I spent an afternoon talking with the Loyers.

"I never start something I don't finish," said Joe Loyer, still lean and wiry at 67. "I've been here, and I'm going to be here."

We walked through the old barn, now used only for storage, and around the quiet farmyard. "When we began, this was just solid forest and cold ground. The soil required such nutrients as nitrogen and phosphorus. In the early days, vegetables and hay would grow, but the yield was too small to market. After maybe ten years of clearing the trees and plowing and fertilizing the ground year after year, the earth gradually warmed enough and became productive enough to give us good crops, especially hay for the cows. Both my wife's family and mine were Michigan pioneers, and now we've helped settle Alaska. And let me tell you, it was a long way from being easy and a long way from being a handout. We came in on a contract. Nobody had any money in those days, so the government loaned us enough to live on. And we paid it back, every penny.

"People who come to Alaska need a little training. You've got to know how to begin or else you'll make a mess of everything and probably freeze to death to boot. This is rugged country," he emphasized. "You've got to be able to handle pretty near anything."

It was now well into October and

Wild eyes glare from a traditional ceremonial mask carved in birch by Aleut Fred Anderson. Eskimo craftsman Junior Slwooko fashioned the seabird from walrus ivory.

winter was settling in; the season, Joe Loyer said, "that pushed out many of the original settlers."

Ice had begun to form on streams and rivers. Waterfalls were frozen in the very act of falling. Snow was inching its way down the mountainsides and into the valleys. In Palmer, people were talking about the coming of "termination dust," as the first snow is called. When snow comes, outside work in the Matanuska Valley halts until the next spring.

Jets of water from a fireboat greet a British tour ship near Cordova on Prince William Sound. Such tour boats complement the state's ferry system, which transports people and freight among the towns on Alaska's roadless coastlines.

Mountains jagged as bear's teeth pierced the sky around Chickaloon, a small town farther up the Matanuska Valley. George gazed at them with appreciation. "Stark and striking," he said, "my kind of mountains." We walked along the banks of the nearly frozen Chickaloon River in a light covering of snow and found bloody tufts of fur from a snowshoe rabbit. Tracks told us the story of a fox catching and killing the hare, and then carrying the carcass back to its den. At another point along the river, bloody ptarmigan feathers stained the snow. We figured that this was the work of a hawk since we could find no tracks. "Lean times are coming," warned George.

A few miles east of Chickaloon, a gigantic tongue of ice flowed down a wide cut in the mountains, stopping just two miles from the highway. Matanuska Glacier, a 27-mile-long ice river, has existed since the Ice Age. We drove to the glacier's towering snout and, after checking our crampons and ice axes, embarked on a climb across its frozen face. We found a world of solid ice: frozen, slippery, hard, lifeless. Randomly sculpted by wind and melt, it glowed with a cadaverous silvery-blue aura. We walked among hills of ice, waves of ice, castles and caves and crevasses of ice. One of earth's most exotic environments, this icescape seemed to me as alien as another planet.

The glacier was totally quiet. In warmer weather it creaks and groans and sometimes cracks with sharp noises like rifle shots. As we walked for hours up and down the mounds of ice, all we heard were the crunching of our crampons and the chopping of our ice axes. Once, however, the wind murmured through the ice beneath my feet. The glacier seemed to be shivering—just as I was.

From the chill solitude of the glacier, we headed by plane to the old mining town of McCarthy and the abandoned Kennicott mining camp nearby. Site of one of the world's richest copper bonanzas in the early 1900's, Kennicott ceased operations in 1938 when the ore played out.

George and I flew in on Halloween in a small airplane equipped with skis; we landed on a runway blanketed with snow. McCarthy dazzled me. It reminded me of a movie-set town for an old Western: Frame buildings lined the unpaved streets. McCarthy has become a cozy hideaway for no more than a dozen permanent residents who exist by hunting, prospecting, trapping, building things—whatever they can find for a livelihood. During the summer, many sightseers come to wander through the town and tour the mine.

That night I went trick-or-treating with Jo Ann Miller and her two youngsters, Greg and Eve, the only children in McCarthy. Jo Ann owns the McCarthy Lodge, a frontier-style hotel with some of the best food in Alaska. Between heaping portions of roast beef and hot biscuits, I asked her about the children's schooling.

"The state has marvelous correspondence courses for children living in isolated places like McCarthy. There's also a free mail-order library. The courses are set up so that any literate adult can teach them."

The next day George and I hiked the four snowy miles to Kennicott. Our guide was Steve Wood, a University of Alaska graduate student who was studying the snowshoe rabbit in the McCarthy area. At Kennicott, we found a beautifully crafted mining camp of barracks, houses, and even a gymnasium and a hospital—all painted a shade of maroon that has weathered well over the years. To my amazement, antiques and other memorabilia lay scattered and untouched in every building: magazines from the 1920's, business correspondence from the 1930's, old X rays, odd-shaped beer bottles with quaint names, a fire extinguisher dated 1914. "Look at them," Steve said, "but *please,* no souvenirs. I know it's hard to resist, but just think how much more exciting this stuff is here in place than in your basement at home."

ON THE FLIGHT OUT OF MCCARTHY, I asked our pilot, Wini Darkow, to head toward 14,163-foot Mount Wrangell. An active volcano, Wrangell was reportedly spouting steam out of newly formed fumaroles. Cheerful Wini, a stocky, powerful man of 48 years, was game and so, it seemed, was our single-engine airplane.

The volcano was visible to the northwest from 50 miles away. Heavy snowfall had smoothed much of the terrain, but the foothills looked stark and forbidding. As we climbed to 13,000 feet, downdrafts gave us a bumpy ride. Approaching the volcano, I spotted seven fumaroles on a high slope. They appeared as dark spots in the snow with plumes of grayish steam swirling above them.

"There's a new ridge exposed on Wrangell's east face," said Wini, pointing. "The volcano's heat has melted a lot of snow." As we flew over that ridge, a sudden severe updraft caught the plane and pushed us to 17,300 feet. Immediately, I started having difficulty breathing. My camera was too heavy to hold. (Continued on page 96)

LAEL MORGAN (ABOVE)

Lone seiner—a salmon-fishing boat—cuts a wake across Prince William Sound southeast of Anchorage. Commercial fishing supports tens of thousands of Alaskans. Off Unalaska, Jan and Stephanie Messersmith gather king crabs; Stephanie flings undersize crabs back to the sea as bearded Jan (right) mans the helm. Prized for their delectable white leg meat, king crabs average eight to ten pounds, with a three-foot leg spread. Trout slung over his shoulder, Danny Boy Snigaroff (above) heads home across the marshes of Atka Island in the Aleutians. The sea provides seasonal work for Aleuts, as commercial fishermen or as workers at canneries throughout the island chain.

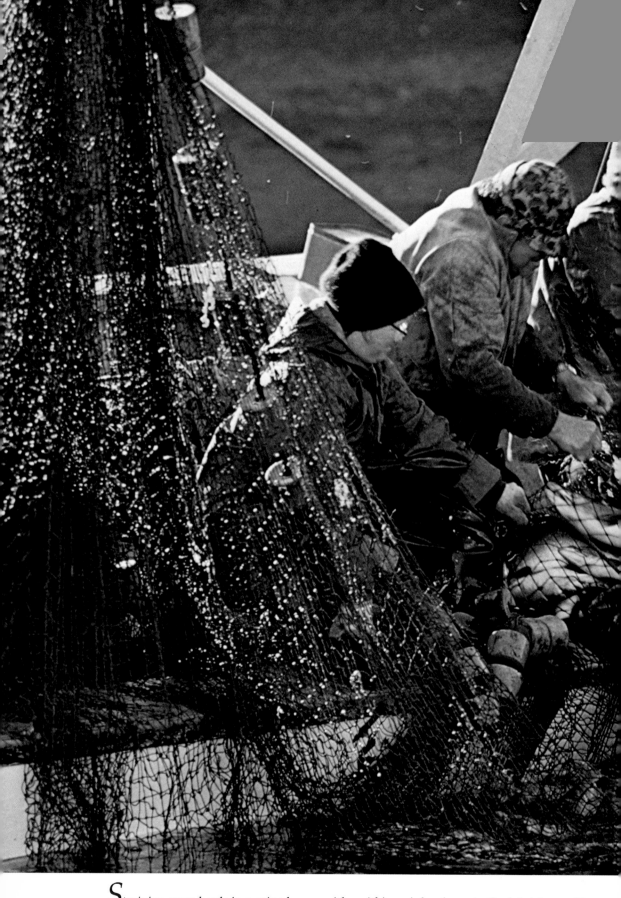

*S*training crew hauls in a seine heavy with writhing pink salmon in Cook Inlet near Homer.

Salmon run Alaska's rivers in late summer and fall, bound for spawning grounds.

*R*ockbound crags of the Talkeetna Mountains jut above a farm in the Matanuska Valley, Alaska's most productive agricultural region. Near his barn and house, a farmer harvests grass for winter feed for his herd of dairy cattle. At lower right, Wayne Bouwens, who owns a nearby farm, pitchforks hay to some of his 43 Holsteins, which produce 300 gallons of milk per day. With his parents, Wayne came to the Matanuska Valley in 1935 as part of a group of some 200 families in a program subsidized by the Federal Government to develop the valley for farming. Many of those original settlers— granted 40 acres each—moved out over the years, but Wayne's family struggled and prospered. He now owns a 120-acre farm, where a third generation of Bouwenses help by tending vegetables in the garden and feeding pigs in the sty.

ALL BY NATIONAL GEOGRAPHIC PHOTOGRAPHER STEVE RAYMER

*W*hisper of scythes brings the fragrance of hay to Old Believers mowing
wild grass near the village of Nikolaevsk. In 1967 this traditional sect of
Russian Orthodox Christians settled on Alaska's Kenai Peninsula with the
hope of finding the religious sanctuary that had eluded them for centuries in
other parts of the world. Today, Nikolaevsk—a community of some 40 rough
spruce cabins, a church, and one street—numbers 300 people, many of whom
have become United States citizens. Villagers work in the fishing industry
—many have built their own fiberglass boats—or in construction trades.
Custom dictates colorful ankle-length dresses and head scarves for women,
beards for men, and daily religious training for the young. Elder Epifan
Reutov teaches Bible studies (far right) each day after school. After a long
day's work and study, evening brings a time of family togetherness (right).

Thunderheads from the earth's interior, gray clouds of steam and ash boil from Augustine Volcano on an island in Cook Inlet. The explosive eruption occurred in January 1976. A violent seismic area, southern Alaska has 40 active volcanoes. A major earthquake on March 27, 1964, devastated Anchorage and leveled Valdez.

GARY GUNKEL

"How're you doing?" called Wini, who seemed unperturbed. I managed to say that I felt very bad. George agreed.

We were banking on our approach to Wrangell's summit—a broad, ice-filled caldera—when we began to lose altitude at a rate of 1,500 feet per minute. The temperature dropped to 20 below zero. What a terrible place to crash, I thought; we wouldn't have a chance.

"Well, we can't make it across the caldera," Wini said casually.

If that's all he's worried about, we aren't in real danger, I decided. Soon the turbulence subsided and there was ample oxygen. I, for one, was happy to be alive.

Before we landed, Wini spotted some caribou on the tundra, and we flew close enough to see them without stampeding the herd. The animals, some with huge branching antlers, were engrossed in their search for food and barely gave us an upward glance.

Back safely on the ground, George and I began to drive south along the trans-Alaska pipeline right-of-way. Road graders, dump trucks, crews installing pipe, village-size work camps, and the regal majesty of snow-clad mountains were with us all the way to booming Valdez on Prince William Sound. Once a tiny fishing village, Valdez suffered one major shock in 1964 when a tremendous earthquake and tidal wave swept across southern Alaska and whisked the town away like a chalk mark erased from a blackboard. The thousand citizens of Valdez rebuilt at a new location, but they retained their town's old fishing village, mining camp profile. It remained that way until the early 1970's, when the pipeline—a second shock—came. Indeed, oil development has drastically changed the character of Valdez, the southern terminus of the pipeline and the port where huge tankers will dock and take on crude oil.

From my experience, Valdez is typical of a town bordering a military base. At night, young men come to town from the large pipeline "base" to drink and find female companionship; there are perhaps five bars in town known for their brawls and prostitutes.

The presence of some 4,000 people working on the pipeline's marine terminal, most of them grossing more than $1,000 a week, can only inflate the town's economy. Permanent living quarters are scarce and expensive. Food, clothing, and other goods cost more in Valdez than in Anchorage, but prices in the 49th State have always been much higher than in the Lower Forty-Eight.

George Smyrniotis, formerly of Long Beach, California, was lured to Valdez because he sensed that an opportunity existed there. I was the first customer on the opening day of his Pizza Plaza.

"Valdez will always be a community of families, and that's the kind of restaurant I want, a family one. For now, this is also a pipeline community, but it will evolve into something more stable. This place is like a little Switzerland with all these beautiful mountains; and we also have Prince William Sound. This beautiful scenery will someday draw lots of tourists. I've come because I want to get in on the ground floor of a city just beginning to discover itself."

Alaska's first boom began in the Aleutian Islands some two centuries ago when Russians sailed across the Bering Sea to hunt sea otter. Today sea-otter fur is no longer sought after, and the islands have a different allure —that of wildness and isolation. The Aleutians are also the homeland of the Aleuts, one of Alaska's three distinct Native groups. I made arrangements to visit the islands on the only commercial airline that flies that long and difficult route: Reeve Aleutian Airways.

The founder of the airline, 74-year-old Bob Reeve, is one of Alaska's legendary bush pilots. Crusty, capable, canny—an old bear with a sense of humor—Bob Reeve is the model of Alaskan rugged individualism. Black eye patch over a blind eye, cheap cigar stuck in his mouth, salty Stetson perched on his head, he sits in a swivel chair hung with a .38-caliber pistol and a cartridge belt. He's a man who has always been prepared.

For almost half a century Bob Reeve has flown the airmail in Alaska. He pioneered glacier landings and other rough-terrain techniques. And since World War II, his airline has flown the 1,100-mile-long chain of Aleutian Islands. Generally conceded to be the most dangerous air passage in the world, the Aleutians are known for unrelenting fog, high winds, and mercurial weather.

"Reeve of the Aleutians" is a title that fits him. In just a few weeks, Bob Reeve told me, he was to be inducted into the Aviation Hall of Fame in Dayton, Ohio. Proud as he was of this honor, he seemed even more pleased that he was going first to the U. S. Navy community on Adak, one of the Aleutians, to be present when they officially named the high school there for him.

"Imagine that," he said with a chuckle, "and me a high school dropout!"

Scattered among the 69 islands of the Aleutian archipelago are five of the eleven Aleut villages. Today, there are *(Continued on page 104)*

Rowdy frontier town, Anchorage sprouts tents along its dirt streets in 1915. The city originated in 1913 as a supply center for crews building the Alaska Railroad, a federal project designed to transport coal from mines farther north. By 1940, Anchorage had developed into a quiet city of 4,000 people.

ALASKA HISTORICAL LIBRARY

*B*urgeoning metropolis of Anchorage fills a plain between Cook Inlet and the Chugach

Mountains. Today, 175,000 people—nearly half of Alaska's population—live in or near the city.

ALL BY NATIONAL GEOGRAPHIC PHOTOGRAPHER STEVE RAYMER

*H*ub of Alaska and an international center, Anchorage bustles with activity. On a Saturday morning, shoppers stroll a downtown business district. Alaska's main center for employment, the city draws people from all over the state — including Natives both old and young (left). Tourists and businessmen from other states and from foreign countries — particularly Japan — come to Anchorage, which prides itself as the "air crossroads of the world" (upper, left); Japanese businessmen eat lunch at the airport. "Anchorage has the social and cultural advantages of any city," says a longtime resident, "but its proximity to the wilderness makes it unique."

Decked with October snow, the abandoned mining camp of Kennicott, site of one of the world's richest copper deposits, lies among the Wrangell Mountains. Discovered in 1900 by prospector "Tarantula Jack" Smith, the lode of high-grade ore played out in 1938. Today, the camp attracts tourists visiting nearby McCarthy—once a supply center for the mining operation, and now home to a dozen permanent residents. Still clutching her candy the morning after Halloween, five-year-old Eve Miller, one of only two children in McCarthy, peers from the front doorway of McCarthy Lodge, owned by her mother, Jo Ann. A sign outside the lodge helps keep the peace.

only about 2,200 Aleuts; once they numbered 20,000 people, but, during the 18th century, their culture was shattered when they were invaded and subjugated by Russian fur traders. World War II further reduced their population: Many Aleuts were forced to evacuate their homes; others were imprisoned or killed by the Japanese. A major land battle—the only one fought on North American soil—took place on the Aleutian Island of Attu. The battle for Attu, now deserted except for a small contingent of U. S. Navy and Coast Guard personnel, claimed the lives of 2,899 men, 549 of them Americans.

I booked passage on Reeve Aleutian Airways to Unalaska; its population of 500 makes it the largest community in the islands. Like most of the original Aleut settlements, Unalaska is located on the north side of its island, facing the Bering Sea, which is richer in fish and sea mammals than the Pacific Ocean to the south. Unalaska was an established Aleut community when the Russians arrived about 1765. Today, the Russian legacy lingers among the Aleuts. Most have Russian surnames; much of their food is prepared in Russian style; and their religion is Russian Orthodox Christianity. A large, 150-year-old church with an onion-shaped dome dominates the weathered frame houses of Unalaska.

I asked newly elected city council member Vince Tutiakoff to tell me about Aleut culture and its importance to the community. "An obvious answer would be to say that our culture is trying to survive and an example of this is that the Aleut language is taught in school," Vince said. "But the most important thing is that we *know* we are Aleut. Why? Because we live here, in *our* islands, like our people have for thousands of years. The sea and its animals, the winds, the isolation of the islands, our family life: This is our culture. If you are Aleut, you are affected very deeply by these things, and you know them; they are a part of you."

Although Unalaska is a treeless island, the Native village corporation sells lumber that has been salvaged from abandoned military bases. During World War II, large forces of men were stationed on Unalaska. Until just a few years ago, these ghostly bases were off limits to the people of the island but, under the Native land-claims settlement, the corporation was granted title to them.

Henry Swanson, born 80 years ago on Unalaska to a Swedish father and an Aleut-German mother, spoke to me of the old days—"better days," he claims—around 1900 or so, when the village was "real nice. People kept their weeds cut, and all the buildings were painted and fenced." Henry sat in his small, plain cabin, at a wooden table in the warm kitchen. His clean-shaven face was the color of old ivory, and he spoke quickly, hardly pausing for breath. He had wandered the Aleutians in the 1920's and 1930's, he said. "I just walked the islands and discovered things. In those days, you could lease an island from the Federal Government for $25 a year; big or small, it didn't matter. I raised blue foxes for their fur. Now most of the islands are sanctuaries for birds and marine mammals, and off limits to commercial operations.

"Most of my sailing was done on the Bering Sea, and I tell you, I was lucky I was a good sailor." The old man sat enveloped in the smoke from his ever-present cigarette, his steady blue eyes staring into the past. "One

time, the most horrible waves came. A great undersea eruption had occurred. We were battered for five hours, with waves smashing everything
in sight. They broke the doors and windows out of the pilot house. They
split the lifeboat in half lengthwise. There was no escaping. I had to maneuver the boat so we took the waves broad-
side. At another time, we sailed through
pumice from a volcano; it floated on the
water for as far as I could see. A peninsula
had been created by the pumice on a nearby
island, but later it disappeared. During the
late twenties there was lots of volcanic
activity," said Henry. "Now, they're testing
atomic bombs out near Amchitka."

On one of his explorations in the Del-
arof Islands east of Amchitka, Henry found
an island of the dead. "There was nothing
but skulls and bones on this island. Every-
where I dug I found bones. I remember
finding something very strange, a disk with
writing on it that looked like Chinese. That
was on Unalga Island."

A project organized by Unalaska high
school teacher Ray Hudson was drawing
on the knowledge and memories of Henry
and other elders to help prepare a history of
the island, which Ray was already writing.
The old man was looking forward to his
interview, which was only a week away.
In Unalaska, the past and the future were
becoming important again.

After experiencing the boundless wilderness in Alaska, I found the 20th century
surprising, accidental, even temporary. Arriving in Anchorage from the Aleutians —
or from any isolated outpost — is like landing
on another world. It brings some frustration, some corruption, some future shock,
and in an ironic reversal, a "great adventure," not in the outdoors, but in a city. For
most people, a sojourn in Alaska includes a
stay in the Anchorage metropolitan area,
home to 175,000 Alaskans.

Anchorage: prosperous and roughhewn; churchgoing and whiskey drinking;
the hub and melting pot of Alaska; a buzzing

*Billowing snow flares in sunlight on a ski
slope at Alyeska Resort near Anchorage —
Alaska's main downhill-skiing center.*

American city with crowded shopping centers, blossoming suburban
areas, and a highrise skyline that competes with the regal Chugach Mountains bordering the city. All the stereotypes of the north — the lumberjack,
the homesteader, the rootless hippie, the boomtown hooker, the grizzled

sourdough—are to be found on the streets of Anchorage. But so are sculptors, bankers, actors, civil servants, craftsmen, lawyers, poets, doctors, clerks, and housewives.

Larry Ahvakana, an Eskimo from Barrow who has a bachelor's degree from the Rhode Island School of Design, is artist-in-residence at the Visual Arts Center of Alaska in Anchorage. For the two years before he came to Anchorage, he ran Barrow's first glassblowing studio. "On many days, I would go from whale hunting on the Arctic Ocean to teaching glassblowing," Larry told me. "Now, in this city, I fight traffic and high prices between classes."

Anchorage has undergone amazing growth in the past two decades. I talked with Elmer Rasmuson, Chairman of the Executive Committee of the National Bank of Alaska, about some of the changes. Born in Alaska of Swedish missionary parents and educated as an economist at Harvard, the 67-year-old banker was a leader in Alaska's fight for statehood. And as the decisive mayor of Anchorage, Rasmuson took command after the great earthquake that struck suddenly on Good Friday, March 27, 1964, and led the city to a quick recovery.

The most severe earthquake recorded in North America during this century, the Alaska quake killed 114 people and affected more than 50,000 square miles in the south central part of the state. In Anchorage, streets dropped as much as 30 feet, roads buckled, buildings cracked, bridges collapsed, and whole neighborhoods were devastated.

Now, 12 years later, Elmer Rasmuson is still helping to guide the city through the difficult times of an abnormally inflated economy. He spoke optimistically about the future. "Anchorage has excellent port facilities. It's the air crossroads of the world, and it serves as the trade and service center for two-thirds of the state's population. Look at the wealth of natural resources it can draw on for industrial growth: tremendous supplies of coal, lumber, and fresh water.

"And now that the Alaskan Natives have received their rightful stake in this capitalistic world of ours, we will be looking to them to provide a new strength in the development of our land and its resources. As I see it, our prospects for healthy growth have never been better."

Among Alaskans of long standing, I often heard it said that the "real Alaska" is not to be found within the limits of any city. In an obvious way they are right. Alaska's most apparent physical reality is its diverse, awesome wilderness.

From a sidewalk crowded with people on 3rd Avenue in downtown Anchorage, I looked north beyond the storefronts, beyond the traffic, beyond the tall buildings. Clearly etched on the horizon, I saw 20,320-foot Mount McKinley rising some 130 miles away, and I longed to be back out there, in Alaska.

Fluted walls of an ice cave frame author Fred Kline on Matanuska Glacier, a 27-mile-long river of ice northeast of Anchorage. Meltwater carved the cave and sculpted the daggerlike shaft of ice near its mouth. Glaciers blanket some 20,000 square miles of Alaska. They form at high elevations receiving heavy snowfall; pressure of the snow's own weight gradually turns it to ice.

A PUNGENT STEW OF LYNX MEAT simmered on a wood-burning stove inside the log cabin. From the ceiling hung a kerosene lantern that filled the room with soft shadows. Lively conversation and easy laughter seemed to mellow the awesome silence of the arctic night.

"I don't have parking problems. I don't have utility bills. If I'm out of water or wood, it's my fault," said Helen Zuray, a petite young woman who had left Boston to settle along the Tozitna River, 35 long wilderness miles from the nearest village, Tanana, deep in Alaska's interior.

Stan, Helen's husband, had turned his back on college and a 40-hour workweek to homestead five acres of state land. "I get a certain sense of satisfaction from knowing that I built my own home, that I bring in my own meat. There's a direct relationship between the work I do and the benefits I receive," he told me as he poked another log into a stove crafted from a 55-gallon oil drum. "When I think of all those people back in civilization, working full time, pouring all their loot into houses and cars, I'm convinced I'm better off. If I'm a dropout, I've dropped into something better. I've found a pleasant way to live."

For three years, Helen and Stan, both in their 20's, have lived in the wilderness; but it has not been easy. As we washed dishes with water stored in a plastic garbage can, Helen told me about the time they were so hungry they were forced to eat their sled dogs. In the first months, fire destroyed all they owned except for a toolbox with an ax and a bow saw. Later, a grizzly bear knocked Stan out of a tree into the river, mauling his arm before inexplicably lumbering away.

"Helen cried a lot in the early days," recalled Stan, a short, slender man with a quick smile. "She wanted to stay in the tent and prepare nice meals. I told her we wouldn't make it that way."

So with stamina and determination, Helen learned to butcher bear and moose, to haul logs by dogsled, to split spruce for firewood, and to launder clothes in a bucket. Now at home in the wilderness, beside a sparkling river where salmon spawn, Helen enjoys the tranquillity and beauty at her doorstep—the fragile, fleeting rainbow of tundra flowers and the awesome splendor of northern lights shimmering with color above a land barely touched by man.

My visit with the Zurays was one of the stops on my journey through the interior—the immense sprawl of land that lies between the Alaska and Brooks ranges. Most of it remains a roadless wilderness of somber spruce forests, grassy bogs, and rolling alpine tundra. Great meandering rivers

Balanced precariously in midair, a tobogganer tests his skill on a snow slope in Ruby, an isolated village along the Yukon River. In winter, such games break the routine of trapping and chopping firewood. Most towns of the interior—an empty land bounded on the south by the Alaska Range and on the north by the Brooks—line two major rivers, the Yukon and the Kuskokwim.

and Lonely Land
By Cynthia Russ Ramsay

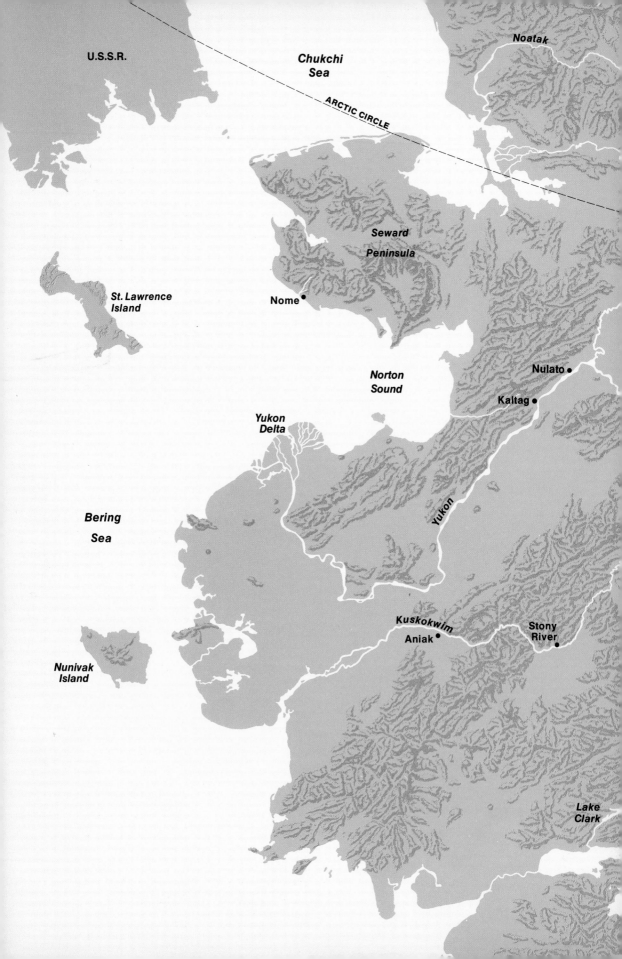

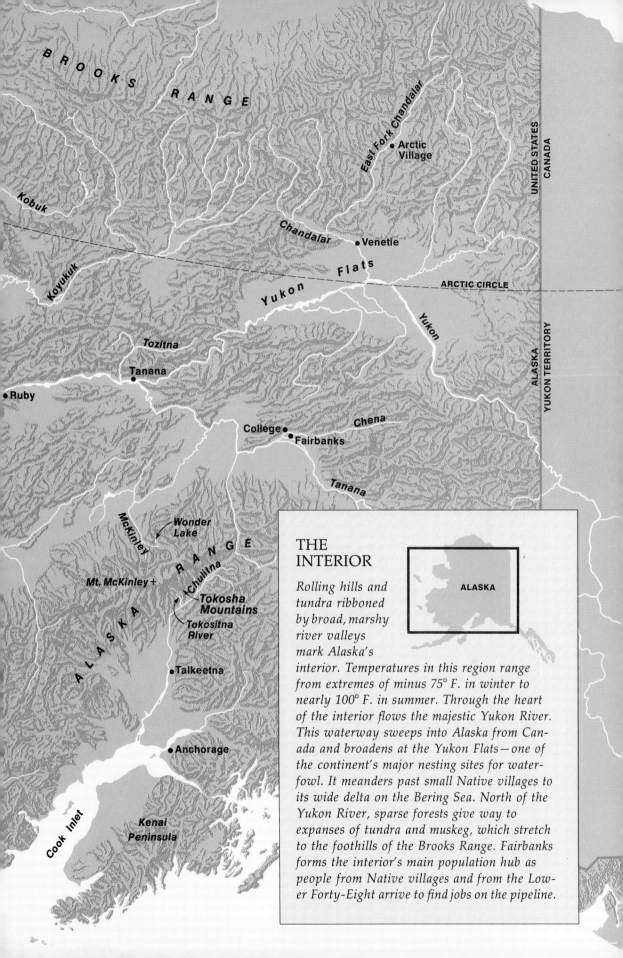

B R O O K S   R A N G E

Kobuk

Koyukuk

East Fork Chandalar

• Arctic
  Village

Chandalar

• Venetie

Yukon   Flats

ARCTIC CIRCLE

Yukon

UNITED STATES
CANADA

ALASKA
YUKON TERRITORY

Tozitna

Tanana

• Ruby

College
• •
  Fairbanks

Chena

Tanana

McKinley

Wonder
Lake

A L A S K A   R A N G E

Chulitna

Mt. McKinley +

Tokosha
Mountains

Tokositna
River

• Talkeetna

• Anchorage

Cook Inlet

Kenai
Peninsula

THE INTERIOR

ALASKA

*Rolling hills and
tundra ribboned
by broad, marshy
river valleys
mark Alaska's
interior. Temperatures in this region range
from extremes of minus 75° F. in winter to
nearly 100° F. in summer. Through the heart
of the interior flows the majestic Yukon River.
This waterway sweeps into Alaska from Canada and broadens at the Yukon Flats—one of
the continent's major nesting sites for water-
fowl. It meanders past small Native villages to
its wide delta on the Bering Sea. North of the
Yukon River, sparse forests give way to
expanses of tundra and muskeg, which stretch
to the foothills of the Brooks Range. Fairbanks
forms the interior's main population hub as
people from Native villages and from the Lower Forty-Eight arrive to find jobs on the pipeline.*

—the Yukon and Kuskokwim—form major waterways to the Bering Sea. Most villages in the interior are on their banks.

At the southern edge of the region stands 20,320-foot Mount McKinley, North America's highest peak, towering above a chaos of ice, snow, and rock. In another enclave, thousands of lakes, streams, sandbars, and islets form a 180-mile-long basin called the Yukon Flats, which provides a summer haven for some two million waterbirds. Throughout the entire far-flung region, the climate is remarkably uniform—bone-numbing, sub-zero weather much of the year, but with temperatures that soar well into the 90's during the brief summer.

I saw the interior in what must be the most beautiful times of year: in March, when days usually warm up to zero, but it is still cold enough to produce the lovely sound of snow crunching underfoot; and in October, when the willows, birches, and marsh grasses ignite the land with red, yellow, and gold, and the scourge of mosquitoes and flies has surrendered to the frost.

For thousands of years, Athapascan Indians roamed the interior, fishing for salmon in summer and hunting moose and caribou in winter. By the 1930's all the nomadic bands had settled into villages.

About 80 percent of Alaska's population has come to the state since 1940. Some people came, like the Zurays, in search of a new life-style. David Hassinger came to Aniak from Minnesota at age 40 with his wife and two teenage sons. He moved north, he said, because he found himself making too many payments on too many things he didn't need.

Jerry Davis, who has driven a taxi in Fairbanks for 13 years, said, "Lots of guys save up for a year to go fishing. I can go anytime, and I can hunt and trap if I want."

Some people came to escape crowds and pollution, others simply with the hope of making money. Military construction during World War II and the Korean war brought men looking for jobs to Fairbanks, but nothing like the recent flood of people lured by work on the pipeline.

And to the interior, as to the rest of Alaska, came men like Jimmy Beaver. "I made an extended trip to Alaska, and I liked it so well I forgot to go back," he told me with a wink.

MOST OF THE INTERIOR remains a hinterland beyond roads. Whenever I could, I packed my sleeping bag and some emergency rations of chocolate and nuts, left the trampled snow of Fairbanks, and boarded a plane for one of the backcountry villages. And at the end of each village street, in back of the last house, I always found the wilderness, a harsh, unforgiving land that still takes the measure of a person—as it did with Marius Hofseth.

Maury was riding a snowmobile down the frozen Kuskokwim one day a few years ago. His rifle began to slip off the machine, and he grabbed for it. Somehow he caught his hand in the treads. Although he struggled desperately, he couldn't free it. With the temperature 25 below zero and getting colder, Maury rolled up his sleeve to numb his arm, then reached for the ax on the snowmobile runner. With one stroke, he chopped off his hand. And then he walked more than a mile to the nearest miner's cabin. "What else could I do?" Maury asked with a shrug.

"You've got to know what you're doing out there. You don't make many mistakes and come back," said John Swenson. His 92 years gave a special weight to his words.

I spent an afternoon in Tanana listening to John in his tiny cabin with its sagging cot and dozens of children's drawings decorating the wall. John came to Tanana as a serviceman in the U. S. Army in 1913, and has lived there ever since. In summer he would fish the Yukon and cut wood for the steamboats running on the river. In winter he would go out with his dog team for weeks at a time, hauling mail, inspecting the telegraph line, and leading survey teams.

"I also kept on the go trapping," he said, peering at me through the dim light. Although the village had electricity, John had no use for it, preferring to read by flashlight. "I loaded up the sled with enough dry fish for myself and the dogs to exist on for a couple of weeks. With my gun, I could pretty well live off the country. You can eat almost anything. I've eaten crows and owls, but I never was partial to porcupine. Most things are good enough, though. It's all in the head.

"Many a time I had to sleep out at 50 below zero. But a sleeping bag is a pretty warm thing. And you can always dig a shelter in the snow with a snowshoe as a shovel. Spruce boughs keep the snow out and make a fine mattress too. The worst part is getting up in the morning."

John brought to life for me a vanished era of big-hearted and big-muscled men, the freewheeling sourdoughs who took risks and tested their strength, all in a day's work. Although now gaunt and feeble with age, John walks down to the store every morning at nine and buys a supply of candy, gum, and soft drinks for his grandchildren and great-grandchildren who come by to chop wood, shovel his walk, and keep him company.

"I know I'm going to die soon. But I've had a good life, and I can't complain. I just hate to leave the kids."

John had married twice, both times to Athapascan women, and half of the village of Tanana is related to him—including Johnny Folger, a young man who had just committed suicide at age 27.

Virtually the entire village of 450 people turned out for a potlatch—a ceremonial feast held in memory of Johnny. The town hall was packed. People sat on benches along all four walls and in rows on the floor. Caldrons of moosehead stew, boxes with chunks of roast moose, and narrow cartons of pilot bread—a hard biscuit—were offered to each person by Johnny's family. Later, youngsters came around with cookies, cans of fruit, sticks of gum, and packets of butter. No one refused anything, for it would have been unspeakably rude. Everyone brought paper bags to carry away what they could not eat.

After the meal and a simple eulogy, music began. A drummer beat a slow, halting rhythm. Three women sitting beside him chanted softly. Soon the singing and drumming drifted into a stronger, bolder cadence. Two girls wearing jeans moved to the center of the floor and started to dance in an easy, rolling shuffle. Slowly, a few at a time, more people joined them. Bolts of cloth were unfurled and tossed to the dancers, who held the swirling cascades of color as they swayed and circled.

The dancing lasted far into the night—a communal tribute to the dead man, and a solace of fellowship to the living. Johnny Folger's suicide was not an isolated tragedy; in the last 15 years the suicide rate among Alaskan Natives has tripled. Alcoholism is also a big problem. Both are born of the same frustration and discontent.

Glenn Gregory, a lean man who runs an air-taxi service and owns a grocery store in Tanana, drew upon his 30 long years in the interior to explain to me the causes of such despair. "The problem started with the breakdown of the traditional life, and with the pressure on families to send their children to school," he said, ushering me into his spacious living quarters in the back of the store.

"Instead of taking his whole family out on the trapline as he once would have, the man left his wife and children behind in the village. Then the welfare workers started coming around. To them the cabins looked impoverished and bare of food. The outsiders didn't know of the meat cache out back, or that Indians buy food only as they need it. When the husband returned from his trapline, he found that his wife took in more money from welfare just sitting at home than he made working his head off trapping.

"What incentive did the man have to go on? At the same time it bothered him and injured his strong sense of pride to accept welfare. He got to drinking. Then he drank some more, partly because there wasn't much to do. Then he felt ashamed and drank again.

"Now take Johnny Folger," he said, running his hand through his short-cropped white hair. "He did a little dog mushing, but otherwise he had no interests. Twenty years ago, he would have been kept very busy out on the trapline."

Bertha Demoski, a soft-spoken woman from Ruby, a village down the Yukon, explained it another way. "It is no good for a young man to live with his mother and have no job."

I flew to Ruby, a former gold-rush town, under a leaden sky. A gray stubble of birches lined the white swirl of the river, while the rest of the landscape was a tapestry of black trees and white snow.

I dropped my pack in Harold and Florence Esmailka's store. Over a savory moose hash and many cups of coffee we talked about changing times. "Ten years ago 75 percent of the store trade still depended on barter in wood, fish, and furs," said Harold, a slight, energetic man who also operates his own air-taxi service. "But we haven't had a good woodpile in front of the store for six years. There's no barter now; people don't have to cut wood or trap. Too many people lean on welfare. There's a few who need it and a lot who don't."

Harold told me that someone just the other day had stolen supplies and a rifle, which he kept in a cabin on his trapline. "That never would have happened before. We always left the cabin door unlocked for anyone who might need shelter. If anyone used the cabin, he always left wood so the next guy could start a fire. Property was respected. That was the law of the Yukon."

Florence interrupted to feed us again. She brought out a jar of "squaw candy"—chewy strips of salmon soaked in brine, then smoked—a delicacy now, a special treat for those who still take the time to prepare it.

"Jobs are scarce in the villages," Harold continued, "and to find a job a

Ridges of rock and snow confront climbers nearing the summit of lofty Mount McKinley—at 20,320 feet North America's highest peak. Because of violent storms, climbs of McKinley can last up to three grueling weeks.

man has to leave. But coming from the village, he is not geared to a nine-to-five job. If he takes time off for celebrations back home or to go hunting and fishing, he may get fired."

Where the future will take the Athapascans is not clear. There is a new pride in being Native, and with it a determination to keep the Indian heritage alive. Schools are beginning to teach the Indian language; the traditional methods of hunting, fishing, and trapping; and the skills of tanning, beadwork, and making snowshoes, dogsleds, and birchbark canoes.

But the land-claims settlement—with its far-reaching, complex provisions for land, cash, and royalties—plunges the Indian headlong into the world of high finance and accelerates the pace of change.

Some 9,200 Athapascans are stockholders in Doyon, Ltd., the Native-owned regional corporation established by the settlement act. With its tremendous resources that will include 12 million acres of land and payments of 120 million dollars over ten years, Doyon can become a powerful instrument in shaping the Indians' future.

That future rests in the hands of leaders like John Sackett, popular and dynamic chairman of Doyon, and Alfred R. Ketzler, president of the Tanana Chiefs Conference, Inc.—a social-service organization—and one of the men who lobbied most strongly in Congress for the settlement act. Even though politics and corporation business take both men far from their villages, they retain strong emotional ties to their land and people. Thus far, the directors of Doyon have moved more cautiously than some of the other corporations in making investments.

"We spent a lot of time selecting the (Continued on page 122)

*B*ewildered newcomers looking for jobs and apartments wander down honky-tonk Second Avenue in Fairbanks. Others (below, left) wait in long lines with their luggage at an airport rent-a-car counter. The population of the Fairbanks area—estimated at more than 60,000—has grown by some 20,000 since 1973 because of the rush for pipeline jobs; this rapid increase causes problems such as traffic jams (above). Inflation and insufficient housing can drive the rent for a two-bedroom apartment as high as $750 a month. The cost of groceries (below, right) also soars because of air transportation charges.

*A*ngular spire of concrete juts skyward near the eight-story Ernest Gruening Building on the campus of the University of Alaska in College, four miles northwest of Fairbanks. Named for Alaska's "Father of Statehood" and its first United States Senator, the Gruening Building provides classrooms and laboratories and offices for professors and for research institutes. Anthropology research associate Holly Record (lower, right) teaches undergraduate courses, and studies the culture of the Ahtna Indians with funds from one of the

MARK W. KELLEY (ABOVE)
NATIONAL GEOGRAPHIC PHOTOGRAPHER STEVE RAYMER (BELOW)

many federal grants for Alaska research. The university has branches in nine communities—including Anchorage with a total of 8,500 students—but only the College campus offers living quarters. In 1976, enrollment there rose to 3,000 students, including some 500 Natives. During the Annual Carnival in February, two dormitory teams celebrate the approaching end of winter with a spirited game called "snowball." During fast-moving periods of 15 minutes each, players compete to move the big, lightweight ball across a goal line.

*H*elicopter blades stir a screen of snow for
U. S. Army commandos posing as foreign
forces attacking the trans-Alaska pipeline near
Fairbanks. In "Operation Jack Frost," staged
in January 1976, the Army, Air Force, and
National Guard used 14,000 troops in maneuvers to test the ability of Alaskan forces
to protect the vital oil carrier from enemy
attack. Heavy-laden aggressors advance across

deep snow (upper, right); defenders on snow-mobiles race to intercept them. Helicopter loadmaster David Hendrickson (left) wears a button indicating his pride in Alaska. Despite the recent bonanza of jobs from the development of oil, the biggest single employer in Alaska remains the Armed Forces. Almost 30,000 military and civilian personnel work for the Army, Air Force, Navy, and Coast Guard.

12 million acres. We wanted land likely to have oil and mineral wealth. We also looked at other lands with the eye of the hunter, trapper, and fisherman," said Al Ketzler from behind a broad desk in his modern office at the new Doyon Building in Fairbanks.

"Making money is not our only mission in Doyon," said Al emphatically. "We want to look after the people who wish to live the old way. But we also want to provide training and jobs for those who wish them."

At the time the settlement act passed Congress there were 25 Native villages in Alaska on federal reserves. All but seven joined regional corporations. Arctic Village — 250 roadless miles north of Fairbanks — was one of the seven that gave up its claim to cash in order to gain title to the federal land surrounding it.

"Why?" Lincoln Tritt repeated my question, before replying in slow, measured words. "We can't eat money; we can't make a fire with it. It's the land that provides what we need. Without it we have nothing."

Lincoln, a resolute young Viet Nam veteran with long hair held in place by a headband, is a leader in Arctic Village; he is genuinely concerned for the future of his people. Lincoln is leery of change, even a small change like replacing wooden stoves with oil heaters. "A lot of time here is spent cutting and hauling wood, and when you install an oil stove, you are left with time on your hands."

He recognizes the need to seek legal and professional help. "We don't want to jump into a deal with a mining company and end up with outsiders telling us what to do." He also worries that hunters from the cities are beginning to come to the village. "The hunter who comes in and kills a moose or caribou is taking food from our tables. Then we find they take back only the antlers for a trophy. It's a crime."

Overhead, an engine droned ever-louder as my airplane buzzed the village to announce its arrival. On the three-hour flight back to Fairbanks, the single-engine airplane followed the East Fork of the Chandalar River and then the Yukon in a journey over tundra and muskeg that was endlessly white, with only a scribble of trees marking the snow.

"Drainage navigating. We invented it," ex-pilot Sam White told me later in a voice that still carried the twang of the Maine woods, where he was born 84 years ago. "Had to. We didn't have maps for most of the Alaska Territory when I started flying. Airstrips were scarce, too. We put down on lakes or sandbars in summer and frozen swamps in winter. When the weather closed in, I would put down the first chance I got. I might knock off a ski or a wheel. After a tour in the sticks, I'd come back with the plane laced up with rawhide, a landing gear jury-rigged with hickory from a sled, a wing patched over with canvas."

But Sam never injured a passenger.

In his frame house in Fairbanks, I followed Sam back through the years. He came to Alaska with the U. S. Coast and Geodetic Survey in 1922, when 80 percent of the Territory was unmapped, and stayed because "you didn't have to be bumping shoulders with greedy people all the time." He went on to join the Alaska Game Commission and became the Territory's first flying game warden. Sam cut down on game violations, but they increased when World War II brought military personnel in large numbers.

"They wanted special concessions that would violate the game laws," said Sam, shifting his bulk uncomfortably with the memory of it. Of course, he resigned.

Until he retired at 71, Sam flew the bush, taking care of miners, trappers, fur buyers, survey crews, and anyone in trouble. "The people's bush pilot" he is called, and countless old-timers remember him for the messages he carried, the tobacco he always brought, the pokes full of gold he always delivered.

The change from the past that Sam regrets the most is "the going of the game." The decline in game animals was also a subject of conversation at the Trappers' Fling in Fairbanks—for those of us who could talk above the din of music and laughter. It was a boisterous, happy crowd of some 250 members of the local trappers association and their friends. Women were dressed in evening gowns or slacks, men in well-tailored business suits or flannel shirts and jeans.

Frank James was wearing a sheepskin jacket, a felt fedora, and a red beard, which, he explained, he grew only in winter to keep his face warm. Although Frank had received $260 for a single lynx pelt, it had not been a good season for trapping.

"When the rabbit population is down, the lynx and fox, which prey on them, go down too," said Frank. "And we're in the low year of the ten-year rabbit cycle."

The beaver season had begun, though, and Frank invited me to go with him to his trapline. Next morning, I joined him and his partner Michael Woodward at Frank's home 13 miles south of Fairbanks. I climbed aboard Frank's snowmobile, and we lurched off on a 30-mile trip across the frozen Tanana River, past a series of streams, and through patches of forest; finally, after a bumpy, branch-lashed ride, we shuddered to a halt at the mound of a beaver lodge on the Salchaket Slough.

Earlier in the week, Frank and Mike had towed a chain saw out to the slough. About 20 feet from a beaver lodge, they had cut a hole in the ice, sawing down three feet until they hit water. From a chain they had then suspended the trap, baited with a piece of cottonwood, so that it hung in the water near the beavers' food supply. Since the bait was fresh wood, it would lure the beaver from its own food, which had been underwater all winter. If the beaver took the bait, the trap would close, and the beaver would quickly drown. They had set seven such traps beside beaver lodges along the Salchaket Slough.

The purpose of our excursion that day was to check the traps. Using a long pole with a steel tip, Frank chipped away the thin crust of ice that had formed over the hole and then hoisted the trap. No beaver. He reset the trap, and we rode off to the next one on a winding trail of snow. We passed outcrops of driftwood that looked like silver-gray thunderbolts embedded in ice. We stopped to look at a huge owl, a black shadow atop the skeleton of a birch tree.

"The beauty of the land is half of what makes a trapper," said Frank.

Perhaps that explains why Frank and Mike seemed little bothered by their lack of luck that day. The subject of wolves drew a much stronger reaction. "I didn't get a moose this year, nor did my brother," said Frank.

"Part of the problem is overhunting the moose. But I found moose on my trapline killed by wolves. What it boils down to is there's not moose enough for both hunter and wolf."

Everyone agrees that the number of moose has dropped sharply in the Fairbanks area. Three explanations are offered for the decline: attack by wolves and other predators, overhunting by man, and unusually severe winters with heavy snows that have blanketed the willows—the moose's main winter food. The Alaska Department of Fish and Game has developed a wolf-control program that has hunters stalking wolves from the air. Conservation groups are extremely critical of this program.

While such environmental groups seek to block the wolf hunts in the courts, the Department of Fish and Game has proceeded with its program, killing a hundred wolves during the winter of 1976. The spring thaw halted the hunters, because they find the wolves only by following tracks in fresh snow. The state has planned to resume the aerial hunts in 1977.

For a further explanation of the problem, I consulted a scientist who has spent the last ten years studying several wolf packs and their prey near Mount McKinley.

Ecologist Gordon Haber believes that wolves are not the problem. "The problem is overhunting by man. In many areas of Alaska, overhunting has so drastically reduced the moose herds that in some cases wolves now are exerting an abnormal impact; but they didn't *cause* the problem. Man and wolf *can* hunt the same herds, but only if man holds his take to reasonable limits." Haber reluctantly agrees that some wolf control may be necessary to undo the results of man's overhunting. But he warns that the control should be far more limited and selective than it is. "Killing wolves at random from the air can fragment a population and result in more hunting units, leading to more killing of moose. And besides, it's a harsh, and to me a pretty disgusting, way to treat such a highly social, intelligent animal."

Bundled against the midwinter cold, 9-year-old Roger McCarty waits to ride a dogsled in Ruby.

Conservation groups in Alaska have suggested that a moratorium on moose hunting be established in the Fairbanks area. This, they believe, will help let nature bring the wolf and moose populations back into balance.

"People won't wait for any of these natural processes to work," said Pat Pyne, "they want moose in their freezers next year." A young, athletic grandmother, Pat took time away from her family in Fairbanks to climb Mount McKinley a few summers ago. A slender, slight woman with fragile features, she has also regularly won the 26-mile cross-country marathon in competition with coeds from the University of Alaska. Pat shares with Sam White and many others in Fairbanks an uneasy concern for what is happening to their hometown.

The town burgeoned when fortune hunters flocked to the banks of the Chena River, where Felix Pedro struck gold in 1902. Through the years, Fairbanks retained the rough edges and live-and-let-live informality of a frontier boomtown. It was a place where the doors of a saloon could swing open in the surge of a brawl, but those same strong arms so quick to fight would help in times of need.

Some of that hearty spirit lingers—just like the mine tailings piled up by the gold dredges outside town. "It's the people who have made Fairbanks a pleasant place," said Pat in her small basement ski shop. "If we feel hemmed in by the cold or bothered by the ice fog, which can last and last, we have our friends. The winters draw us together. But, unfortunately, we're losing that closeness. There are too many people you don't know, too many strangers in a hurry."

And, indeed, the Fairbanks area has grown markedly. Some estimates place the population at more than 60,000—an increase of 20,000 people in just three years. As a result, lines are long at banks and stores; telephone

Load of firewood in tow, an Athapascan Indian in Ruby heads home at dusk. He passes the village clinic along the frozen Yukon—river highway through the interior.

circuits are jammed; and housing is scarce—rents have climbed to as much as $750 a month for a two-bedroom unfurnished apartment. Crime is up, especially auto theft, burglary, and vandalism. Traffic has increased, making air pollution worse, while food prices inflate at a faster rate than in the rest of the country.

"We're hunkering down and waiting for the ones who've come up only for the money to go away—and that should be soon. The old sourdoughs came for gold, but they came for adventure, too," said Pat.

On a hill northwest of Fairbanks stands the University of Alaska, center of wide-ranging Arctic and subarctic research, and the main institution of higher learning in the state. I toured several of the university's research stations on a cold, blustery morning.

Terry Chapin, a plant ecologist at the Institute of Arctic Biology, delves into the wonders of tiny tundra plants. *(Continued on page 136)*

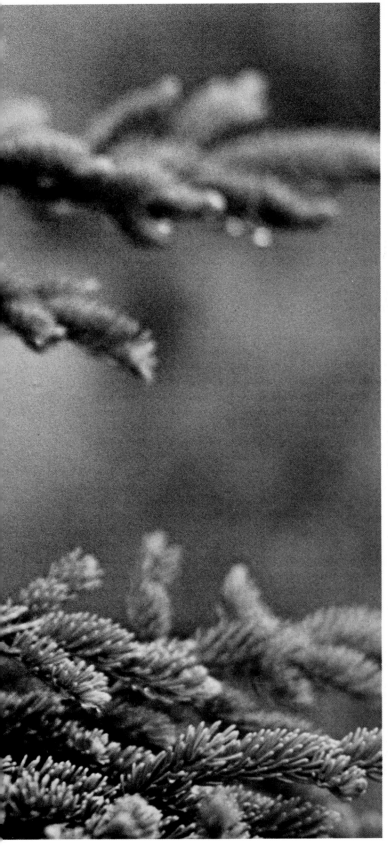

Nibbling a tender cone, a red squirrel crouches among the branches of a white spruce in Mount McKinley National Park. Alaska's brief summers of long, sunny days bring quickened activity to the state's animals and plants. The short growing season still yields a profusion of juicy wild blueberries (below). Wild flowers like the fragrant Jacob's ladder (bottom) dot the tundra of Alaska's interior.

Meandering Yukon River flows beneath a bridge built in 1975 to provide all-weather

access to North Slope oil fields and to carry the trans-Alaska pipeline across the river.

*S*weeping the winter sky like streamers, multihued bands of the aurora borealis shimmer above the log cabins of Gold Camp along the frozen Chandalar River. Stars leave bright trails in this time exposure taken on a night when the temperature plunged to minus 58° F. In the lighted one-room dwelling live Johnny Frank (left), 97, a former Athapascan Indian chief, and his 95-year-old wife, Sara. With a couple of neighbors they share a simple subsistence life some 20 wilderness miles from Venetie. For Johnny Frank, the northern lights — charged particles from the sun interacting with earth's atmosphere — blow across the curtain of winter like a wind from heaven.

*P*ushed by a passenger wearing snowshoes, a bush plane equipped with skis for winter swivels into the wind for takeoff at Talkeetna. Survival in Alaska for thousands of isolated people depends year-round on small charter companies, which provide air-taxi service, deliver supplies, mail, and news, and—through their pilots—offer some human contact. In the deep snow covering Pirate Lake near Mount McKinley, a woman wintering in a solitary cabin (right) hurries toward a landing plane. Every couple of weeks, the pilot brings her groceries, heating oil, and mail. Flying small planes in Alaska's unpredictable weather and rough terrain tests the skills of hundreds of bush pilots.

*C*hanting men and dancing women perform the traditional "stick dance" in the Athapascan Indian village of Nulato along the Yukon River. The ritual dance—part of a week-long ceremony honoring the memory of a dead person—can last for 20 exhausting hours. The tall pole, cut from a spruce tree near town, symbolizes a link between the living and the dead. After the dance,

134

NATIONAL GEOGRAPHIC PHOTOGRAPHER BRUCE DALE (BELOW)

villagers carry the pole around the town in an act designed to bring luck to the living. Townspeople — including children (top, right) — then break the pole into several pieces, carry them to the Yukon, and cast them into the river. Athapascans perform the stick dance only in Nulato and nearby Kaltag. A village of 300 people, Nulato houses its post office in a tiny shed (bottom, right).

135

"They freeze at night and in the morning thaw out again and resume growing. They have adapted to the harsh conditions in other ways," he added. "In the tundra, where the sun melts only a thin layer above the permafrost in the summer, plants can't send their roots deep into the ground. So the roots spread out and grow in the shallow blanket of soil."

I also learned that the slightest slope or an altitude change of even fractions of an inch can vary the moisture content of the tundra and make a tremendous difference in the type of plant life that grows.

I stopped at the Geophysical Institute, where scientists launch rockets to probe and gather information on the aurora borealis. "We release barium vapor into space in order to trace the earth's magnetic field, which we believe contributes to the display of lights," explained Dr. Eugene Wescott, a geophysicist. "The earth is constantly bombarded by particles emitted by the sun. When these particles interact with our magnetic field —and particularly with a theoretical double layer about 3,000 miles out— electrons are accelerated. They collide with atoms of oxygen and nitrogen at an altitude of 60 miles, thus creating the fantastic colors and waves."

GEOPHYSICISTS HAVE BEEN SEARCHING for the origin of the northern lights for years. Scientists at the Institute of Arctic Biology were searching for something quite different when they monitored and tested three hardy mountaineers who, in 1967, made the first winter climb of Mount McKinley. They endured adverse conditions, surviving temperatures, with the wind-chill factor, equivalent to a staggering minus 148° F.

The agony of the cold and the ordeal of breathing the oxygen-thin air took a heavy toll and left the men physically weak and mentally sluggish for months afterward. For six days, the men were trapped at 18,000 feet by a howling blizzard with savage winds blowing more than a hundred miles an hour. They stayed in their sleeping bags, huddled in a shallow ice cave which they managed to build, and hung on, waiting for the storm to end. Snowmelt, a handful of raisins and beans, and their will to survive saw them through. "It wasn't too bad, you know," said Ray Genet, one of the three who made that climb. He gruffly disclaimed the agony of the 40-day expedition, and I soon learned that this iron man of fierce determination indeed meant what he said.

Genet looks the impudent character he is. Chunky, dark, exuberant, and immensely strong, he has climbed McKinley 20 times, leading—and sometimes bullying—18 expeditions to the top. His rescue missions on the mountain have made him something of a legend in the state.

He set a more casual pace as we hiked into the Tokosha Mountains, south of the McKinley park boundary, on a chilly October day. We started uphill from wet muskeg that squished and tugged at our boots as we walked, heading for a rocky crest above the high tundra.

Our way became easier as we reached firmer ground where patches of blueberries lured us with their sweetness. But not for long. All conversation ceased as we battered our way through tangled thickets of alder. Finally, ahead of us lay the open tundra, a spongy turf of green lichens called caribou moss.

I asked Genet about his technique of leading mountain expeditions.

"We'll move on in a whiteout, with almost no visibility, even if we have to inch along by compass. Maybe we go just half a mile that day, but it doesn't matter as long as we're moving. It's important to remain physically fit—and it's good for morale. Otherwise people grow restless."

I was beginning to lag.

"We're almost there. You have to push. The extra effort is what builds strength and endurance. Lifting a teacup, even a million times, won't build a bit of muscle."

I was building a big ache in my legs, but I trudged on, and finally made it to the ridgetop, scrambling over rocks dusted with snow in the last couple of hundred feet.

"Why is it so important to get to the top?" I grumbled.

"Because it was the goal we set," he answered solemnly, handing me a chocolate bar. "And, of course, to see what is on the other side," he added with a grin.

We made camp and, after a quick dinner, I drifted into a deep comforting sleep. The next day dawned sunny and clear. The clouds had parted on the great soaring mass of Mount McKinley, thrusting its white grandeur to the heavens. Mighty glaciers descended its flanks and melted into frigid streams aswirl with silt as fine as flour. One of those glaciers, the Tokositna, became the milky green Tokositna River. Genet offered to take me rafting on its fast-moving waters.

"If you fall in, your clothes become heavy with silt," he said, as he inflated a raft with a small pump. "But in an accident the real danger is wearing hip boots. They'll fill with water and immediately pull you to the bottom."

The problem that day was the network of twisting channels that made our way downriver a baffling maze. Constantly changing, the river shifts and cuts new courses almost overnight. Genet was intent on reading the water to find the swifter, deeper main current that would lead us to the Chulitna River and the Anchorage-Fairbanks Highway.

Every bend in the river gave me a different view of McKinley, floating serenely above the lower ramparts of the Alaska Range—an ethereal sculpture against the blue sky. My reverie was interrupted by periodic blunt shouts, "Paddle harder to the left. Harder! Can't you hear?"

We finally arrived at the bridge over the Chulitna and the road to Mount McKinley National Park. A lofty sweep of land, 110 miles from east to west and 35 miles from north to south, the park will more than double in size if the proposed extensions are approved.

Will the proposal of adding 3.1 million acres to the park draw more people—people who will demand more campgrounds, more roads, and better facilities?

Park superintendent Daniel Kuehn indicated that it would; when a national park is created, it is an automatic lure to the public. "We will obviously have to adjust to a heavier load of visitors," he said, "but we hope to maintain the unique wilderness character of McKinley."

When I arrived by ski plane at Wonder Lake, on the northern boundary of the park, the 435,000 visitors who throng the campgrounds, visitor centers, and the park hotel were long gone. Winter had quickly restored the wilderness to the Dall sheep scrambling up improbable cliffs, the moose browsing on willows in the bottomlands, the caribou scooping away the snow with their hooves in search of lichens, and the grizzly bears slumbering in their dens.

In winter five park rangers take turns patrolling the park from Wonder Lake. They patrol by air for the most part, counting game and watching for poachers. But occasionally they use dogsleds. I joined John Haller on such a patrol.

"My job lets the hunters and miners know where the park boundaries are," said John above the wild yapping of the dogs. He was putting them in harness, and like all good sled dogs they were in a frenzy to move out. I held one sturdy, thickly furred dog by the collar as John buckled the animal to the main towline.

"We've got another job now," John said. "Cleaning up McKinley. It's become the highest trash heap in North America. The climbers pack in everything they need. Trouble is, some of them don't bother to pack it out." Snowshoes, crampons, empty fuel cans, tents—the paraphernalia of mountain conquests—litter the climbers' routes.

Finally, the last of the seven dogs was hitched, and we raced across the frozen expanse of Wonder Lake toward the McKinley River. The only sounds were the panting of the dogs and the creaking of the sled. Without breaking their trot, the dogs would grab mouthfuls of snow. I took a turn standing on the runners at the back of the sled—one foot hovering above the jagged teeth of the brake pedal. All I had to do was hang on.

I could lift my eyes and rejoice at the splendor of the mountains, or I could close them and remember the open, honest people who had shared their Alaska with me.

I thought of sourdough Jimmy Beaver who "gets in a good woodpile and rolls with the seasons"—all this simple man asks from life.

I remembered 73-year-old Gusty Mikhael who lives in the tiny village of Stony River. Half-Athapascan, half-Eskimo, Gusty hopes to beat his bad luck beaver hunting by finding gold—in order to buy his grandchildren an airplane.

There was also Glenn Fredericks, a shrewd university graduate who wants to help the Indians and Eskimos who live along the Kuskokwim by bringing industry to his homeland.

As I sped by dogsled across the crystal snow on McKinley's flank, I reflected that it is a combination of the people and the land of the interior that makes this region of Alaska so special to me. I had found beauty in nature and grace in humanity; but I also had found discontent and a stirring of change. No matter what happens, I decided as the cold stung my face, I plan to return in a few years, and I hope to find intact the free spirit of Alaska's backcountry.

In her snowbound cabin 16 miles from Talkeetna, the nearest town, Carole Bentley stuffs a turkey for Thanksgiving dinner. Four years ago, she and her husband, Bill, came to Alaska from California to find a simpler life close to nature. "It's been hard work," Carole said, "but the rewards of freedom and self-reliance have been unparalleled. We love it here."

NATIONAL GEOGRAPHIC PHOTOGRAPHER STEVE RAYMER

138

5/From the Brooks Range to

NORTH OF THE YUKON, where perhaps 16,000 of Alaska's 400,000 people dwell, there is a single all-weather road to the Arctic Ocean, and that a recent and controversial one. It crosses the great river on a high bridge, reaches the crest of the Brooks Range at Atigun Pass, then descends foothills and stretches of tundra to the oil fields at Prudhoe Bay. For many Alaskans, the haul road constructed by the Alyeska Pipeline Company heralds the long-awaited opening of the north. To others, it is the knife that has finally been plunged into the heart of the last great American wilderness.

There is reason for both views. In one way or another, the Alaskan north, 700 miles broad and 300 miles deep, will develop. Already, there are new hotels in old Eskimo villages and regularly scheduled jet flights to Barrow, Kotzebue, and Nome. There is talk of using the haul road to bring out mineral ores. A new Eskimo government is diligently, but with normal difficulty, trying to establish itself.

And, one way or another, large portions of the wilderness will remain. Some of those seeking it head for the southern slopes of the central Brooks Range, where the Alatna, the John, and the Koyukuk rivers drain the high mountains. Their waters meander through glacier-sculpted valleys rimmed by rocky slopes that thrust high above the tundra. This scene of barren wildness has been proposed as a new national park. Explored and named nearly 50 years ago by Robert Marshall of the U. S. Forest Service, this area is called the Gates of the Arctic. The Gates themselves are formed by the peaks Marshall named Boreal Mountain and Frigid Crags; they frame the broad valley of the North Fork of the Koyukuk. At the nearby confluence of this fast-moving stream and Ernie Creek, Marshall spent a few days, and recorded these simple words in his journal: "We camped between the two rivers on a spot with a view which, we felt, certainly could match the finest in the world."

On a day nearly a half century later I camped in the same spot waiting to rendezvous with a party of backpackers led by Bob Waldrop and including John Kauffmann of the National Park Service. We met in a small grove of spruce where Ernie Creek's clear waters empty into the North Fork and spread curving gravel bars. From a ridge behind the camp, Marshall's marvelous view opened in three directions—to the south, the river valley closed in by the Gates; to the north, the tundra billowing toward distant heights; to the east, the narrow valley of the North Fork shadowed by towering Mount Doonerak. And all of it, as far as I could see, was unmarked by road, smoke, trail, or obvious signs of man.

Clutching a gaff, an intent Eskimo whaler from St. Lawrence Island prepares to snag a slain bowhead whale. By hooking the animal, he and fellow whalers will help steady it in the strong tides of the Bering Sea so that others can butcher it. Eskimos in the Arctic brave treacherous, ice-choked waters in umiaks—walrus-skin boats—to hunt whales and other sea mammals.

the Arctic Ocean

By Joseph Judge

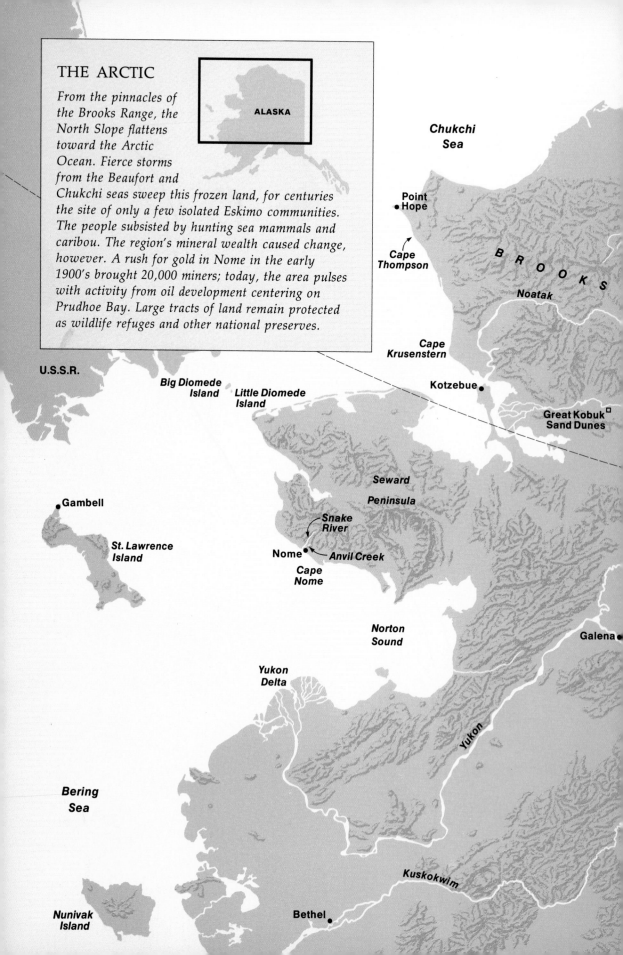

THE ARCTIC

*From the pinnacles of
the Brooks Range, the
North Slope flattens
toward the Arctic
Ocean. Fierce storms
from the Beaufort and
Chukchi seas sweep this frozen land, for centuries
the site of only a few isolated Eskimo communities.
The people subsisted by hunting sea mammals and
caribou. The region's mineral wealth caused change,
however. A rush for gold in Nome in the early
1900's brought 20,000 miners; today, the area pulses
with activity from oil development centering on
Prudhoe Bay. Large tracts of land remain protected
as wildlife refuges and other national preserves.*

ALASKA

Chukchi
Sea

Point
Hope

Cape
Thompson

B R O O K S

Noatak

Cape
Krusenstern

Kotzebue

Great Kobuk
Sand Dunes

U.S.S.R.

Big Diomede
Island

Little Diomede
Island

Seward
Peninsula

Gambell

Snake
River

St. Lawrence
Island

Nome

Anvil Creek

Cape
Nome

Galena

Norton
Sound

Yukon
Delta

Yukon

Bering
Sea

Kuskokwim

Nunivak
Island

Bethel

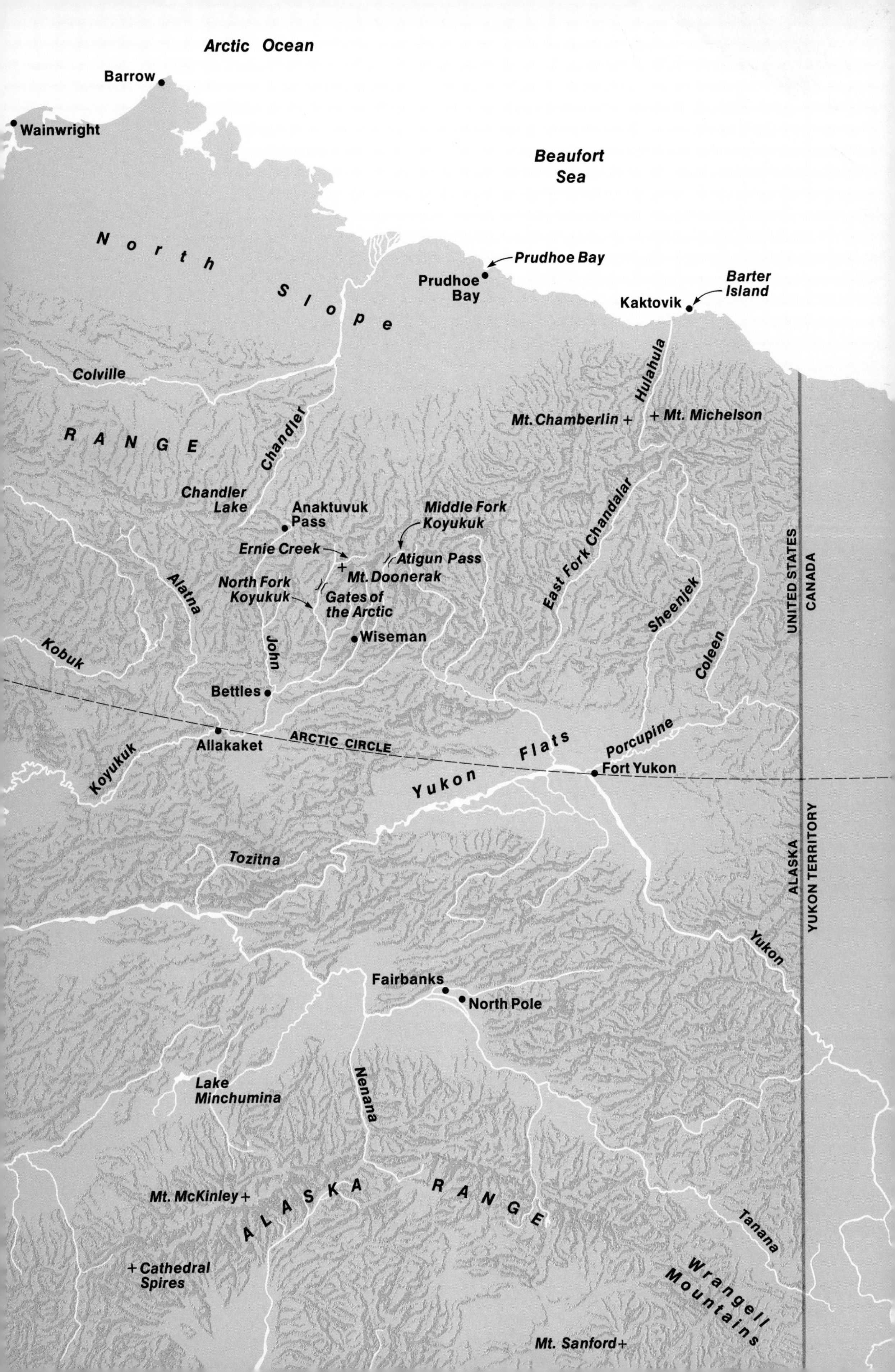

Arctic Ocean

Barrow

Wainwright

Beaufort Sea

North Slope

Prudhoe Bay
Prudhoe Bay

Barter Island

Kaktovik

Colville

RANGE

Chandler

Mt. Chamberlin +   + Mt. Michelson

Hulahula

Chandler Lake

Anaktuvuk Pass

Middle Fork Koyukuk

Ernie Creek

Atigun Pass

East Fork Chandalar

Sheenjek

North Fork Koyukuk

+ Mt. Doonerak

Gates of the Arctic

Alatna

John

Wiseman

Coleen

Kobuk

Bettles

Allakaket

ARCTIC CIRCLE

Yukon   Flats

Porcupine

Fort Yukon

UNITED STATES   CANADA

Koyukuk

Yukon

ALASKA   YUKON TERRITORY

Tozitna

Yukon

Fairbanks
North Pole

Lake Minchumina

Nenana

Mt. McKinley +

ALASKA   RANGE

Tanana

+ Cathedral Spires

Wrangell Mountains

Mt. Sanford +

John, Bob, and I climbed a knoll overlooking Ernie Creek and watched as a cow moose with a calf waded slowly across to feed on willows on the other side. A scene of tranquillity, I thought, a restorative; but I wondered about the future — how many would someday share it?

"How can this be made a national park if only a few intrepid souls can visit it?" I asked John.

"I agree it's unusual and special," he said. "But nowhere in the United States do we have a true wilderness park, a place where a person can go if he feels the need, and lose himself in the wild. There should be such a place. Not everyone is able to see a whale in his lifetime, but it is nice to know that such a thing exists."

During a winter's stay in the Brooks Range, Bob Marshall lived at Wiseman, a collection of cabins built around a roadhouse on the Middle Fork of the Koyukuk. It also formed the setting for his book *Arctic Village*, which describes so memorably the exuberant life of the miners, trappers, and Eskimo families gathered there at the edge of the world.

They are all gone now. The roadhouse has caved in and is lying on its side, and the dozen or so cabins, now used only in summer by hunters, have been abandoned to snowdrifts and silence. But life still flickers in Wiseman in winter; its few inhabitants were stoically waiting out the cold months when I visited there.

I had sent word ahead to my friend Charley Breck via "Trapline Chatter" over station KJNP in North Pole, a town near Fairbanks. A religiously-oriented station, it beams with 50,000 powerful watts over large areas of the bush and conveys, at no charge, messages of every conceivable sort.

When I arrived on the mail plane, Charley's thin, hunched figure appeared down the trail to Wiseman dragging a sled to carry my gear; we were soon snug in his 50-year-old cabin, decked with a four-foot roof of snow. I remarked that the cabin looked to be in good condition.

"Held up by willpower," he said with a grin.

"Anyone else in town?"

"Ross Brockman, Harry Leonard, the Denman family, and the Pasquali family. Two little kids got pneumonia and had to be hauled out for medical attention. Been quiet this winter. A few caribou straggled through. Some workers come in from the pipeline every now and again. You know something — you can walk the few miles over to the haul road and hitchhike to Fairbanks. For the first time ever, people can drive cars in Wiseman!"

The year was slowly turning out of winter, and the period of sunlight was growing slightly longer each day. We watched the soft blue light of evening linger in the lovely valley of the Middle Fork, as white and still as Christmas Eve. "It's as beautiful as ever here, Charley," I remarked.

"Well, I don't feel that I'm looking at a church. I don't fall on my knees when I observe nature. I didn't come up here for beauty. I came up here for freedom."

I had expected that the haul road and a more attractive price for gold would have turned Wiseman, once a center for gold mining, into at least a boomlet town — and jeopardized Charley's freedom.

"There are quite a few miners around in summer, and most of the new interest is in the old placer grounds, because now, with heavy equipment, you can get something out the old boys couldn't handle, and with the haul road, you can bring big machines in.

"This is nugget hunters' country, though, good for small, easy-to-get stakes, jeweler's gold. There's been maybe 16 million in gold taken out of this country. I took nothing. Nobody's found a new creek since I've been here. I was always trying to find something new, but I didn't find a thing, and neither did anyone else. You find enough to keep tempting you, but every creek you explore is another year taken out of your life."

Caribou, not gold, have made the small village of Anaktuvuk Pass, deep in the Brooks Range, famous. It sits on the age-old migratory route of large caribou herds,

Midwinter wish: Weary of the long days of darkness, children in the village of Wainwright etch their sentiments in frost. In the Arctic, the sun never rises above the horizon in December and January.

which each year move from the interior valleys to the North Slope. In 1976 there was considerable consternation and worry because, for the first time in many years, the caribou had not come through Anaktuvuk Pass.

A thin, dry snow was slanting across the flanks of the mountains, and the thermometer had sunk to 30 below as I began walking from the airstrip to the village. A large, smiling Eskimo woman in a flowered pink parka appeared in a cloud of snow, packed me aboard her snowmobile, and drove me clattering and clanking over the hard ground to town.

Later, I walked out under an incredible display of stars and drank in again the lonely beauty of the far north. Several young hunters, in search of caribou, were moving down the valley on their snowmobiles on a 90-mile trip to Chandler Lake, where a small herd was wintering.

There is serious concern that something drastic has happened to the caribou herd upon which Anaktuvuk Pass depends. An aerial census made in 1970 indicated a population of 240,000 animals; in 1976, some estimates were as low as 30,000, although the official count was 58,000. The great numbers of caribou that used to winter near Bettles were not there. Apparently no caribou migrated through Anaktuvuk Pass in 1976 because there were none to migrate through.

There are many theories to explain the problem. Some people think simply that the surveys are inaccurate; others believe that research will show that the herd of wandering animals periodically fluctuates in size; another theory I heard discussed blamed (Continued on page 160)

145

Stalking sea mammals with a rifle, a St. Lawrence Islander scans the ice-crusted Bering Sea while his partner maneuvers their motor-powered umiak toward open water. Propelled by a light breeze, a group of Eskimo whale hunters heads toward shore in a small sailing umiak. Electric lamps pierce the darkness of an April night as hunters butcher a whale at the edge of the shore ice near the village of Gambell on St. Lawrence Island. Long-handled flensing spades quickly slice away skin and inches-thick blubber and carve out large chunks of meat. The raw skin and a layer of blubber make an Eskimo delicacy called muktuk. *An entire village benefits from every whale kill—the hunters distribute the meat among all the families living there.*

Rippled by Arctic winds, Great Kobuk Sand Dunes rise a hundred feet above a tributary of

the Kobuk River. The 350 square miles of sand in this region originated from glacial silt.

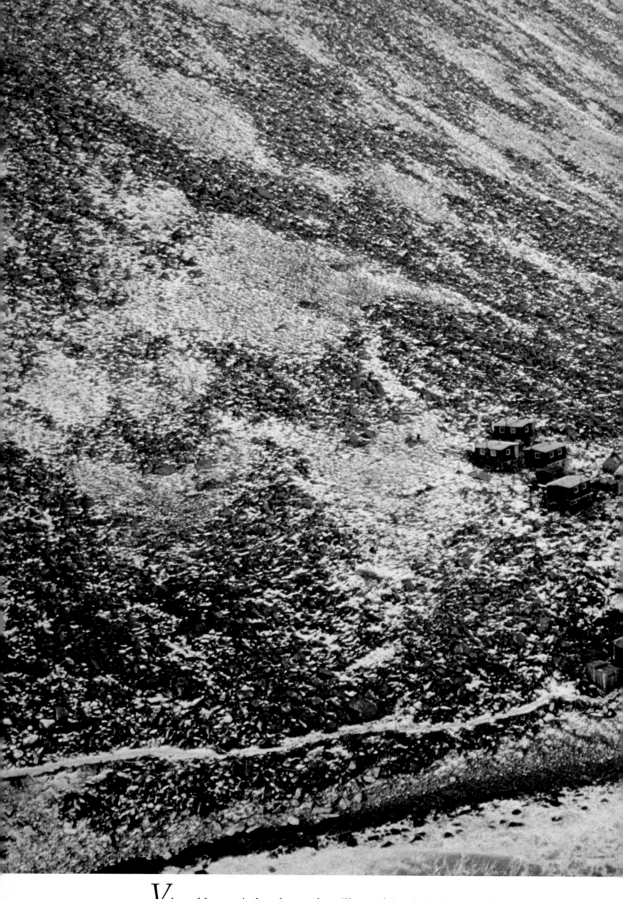

*V*ulnerable to wind and sea, the village of Ignaluk clings to the steeply plunging

cliffs of Little Diomede Island. Winter storms isolate the tiny settlement for weeks at a time.

*L*owering mist engulfs a monstrous gold dredge near Nome—site of a stampede of 20,000 prospectors in the early 1900's. The rising price of gold has reactivated mining in Nome. This dredge digs underwater with a continuous chain of buckets, which dump gravel into a hopper inside the dredge. There, a high-pressure spray separates the gold from the coarser material; the gravel then rides a conveyor belt up the protruding arm and falls into tailings. In 1975, this dredge, owned by the Alaska Gold Company, scooped up more than a million tons of gravel for a yield of just 556 pounds of gold. Dredge operator Earl Anderson compares his work to driving a car. "You're constantly watching many things at the same time," he said. "But the hard part is the hours you put in." An electrician (above) smiles as his ten-hour shift ends.

Chanting Eskimo musicians beat a rhythm on drums made of whale stomach during the

Spring Whaling Festival at Point Hope. This ceremony honors the whale and seeks its goodwill.

ROLLIE OSTERMICK (BELOW)

*S*haggy musk-oxen thunder through snow during a roundup at the Nunivak Island National Wildlife Refuge. The present herd of 700 has grown from 31 Greenland animals released in the 1930's; the native stock became extinct in the 1850's. A tranquilized polar bear near Barrow shields her cub as she awaits tagging by biologists. An Arctic fox howls in the wild. Its long coat turns white in winter.

157

Twilight shadows veil rumpled slopes of the eastern Brooks Range. In this remote realm lies

the Arctic National Wildlife Range, which protects caribou, musk-oxen, and Dall sheep.

the decline on the "snow go." Parties of hunters can now make quick, one-day trips to herd locations, the snowmobile having effectively doubled their range. For some hunters, stalking has given way to chasing and herding by machine. But shots fired into a milling herd result in crippled and wounded animals — and a great increase in waste.

Some hunters today often leave their mistakes behind and bring home only the nice, fat, well-shot cow. They can keep shooting until they get what they want, leaving the rest for the wolves and ravens. Perhaps because of the snow go, there are more unnecessary kills and, therefore, fewer caribou.

Most significant changes in the far north can be dated to the big strike at Prudhoe Bay. One of the lasting effects is the confirmation of Barrow as the political capital of the region. It is the headquarters not only of the Arctic Slope Regional Corporation and the village Ukpeagvik Inupiat Corporation — one of the three largest in all Alaska — but also of a new government, the North Slope Borough. It is the largest in extent of any political subdivision in the United States, and one of the most intriguing experiments in self-government anywhere.

I have powerful memories of my first visit to Barrow a few years ago: the murk of the midwinter sky shutting out what little light penetrated a cloud of ice fog; ghostlike figures walking a bleak landscape; eating caribou steak in Al's Cafe; hearing Beatles music on a jukebox; visiting the Polar Bear movie theater, which had been converted into a dance hall and general free-for-all. Barrow at that time reminded me of a bunch of packing crates flung ashore in a gale and left on the rim of the Arctic Ocean.

Time on her hands, a woman in Gambell sits beside an electric sewing machine in deep winter. Life in the harsh Arctic has taught the Eskimo patience and quiet reserve.

During a recent visit, I found that Barrow had boomed and then some. The one-room airport terminal was jammed with a diversity of people who seemed out of place — an oil lawyer from Texas, a corporation lawyer from

Seattle, a hotel manager from Anchorage. The historic Top of the World Hotel had been devoured by flames, as had Al's Cafe. A 40-room Sheffield Hotel, flown to Barrow in modular units by cargo plane and then sledded into town, now handles overnight visitors.

This forthright exhibit of free enterprise summarized some of the things Barrow Eskimos think about these days — in addition to whales and polar bears and caribou. The hotel was assembled by Eskimo, Inc., a subsidiary of the village corporation. Sheffield, an Alaska hotel chain, manages the building, owned jointly by the village corporation and Tundra Tours, Inc., a subsidiary of the regional corporation.

Next to the old Presbyterian Church, a handsome new borough administration building has risen. Its open, four-story interior is carpeted in a rich red color, and office floors are suspended from interior pilings. The building is almost awe-inspiring considering its location and the amount of heat it must gulp down at temperatures of 30 below zero.

Barrow also has a new department store that would be right at home in any American suburb. It is owned by the village corporation.

Inevitably, there was a reaction to all this plush development — particularly with the new hotel — by a group of young, idealistic Eskimos. They painted hateful signs on the front of the hotel, caused problems in the bar until it had to be closed, and announced their discontent with a "honkie hotel" that took profits out of their town and made little visible attempt to train young Natives for jobs in the hotel's administration. The Sheffield management has denied this charge and shows clear evidence that it has been trying.

Mike Monchino, a young man from New Jersey who was managing the hotel, explained, "It's difficult to find anyone to work for $6 an hour when jobs in town are going begging at $13 an hour."

I had traveled to Barrow to attend the second annual meeting of the regional corporation, to be held in the all-purpose room of the local school. Joe Upicksoun, president of the corporation, and Larry Dinneen, executive director, discussed with me a multimillion-dollar agreement they had reached with Standard Oil of California, Union Oil of California, Texaco, and Amoco. "These are exploration contracts only," Mr. Upicksoun told me. "We want to know what's in the ground, and where, and so do they. We want to get some idea of what we are going to be worth so we can plan intelligently."

An intelligent plan put forward by Eben Hopson, long a power in Eskimo politics, was to form the North Slope Borough. Realizing that a political entity with taxing powers could perform needed social services while a profit-making corporation could not, Hopson — now mayor — forged such a unit encompassing virtually the entire North Slope. The borough began with a levy of nearly seven million dollars in taxes against the oil companies and their property. The companies protested the legality of the arrangement, but the Alaska Supreme Court upheld the new government and its taxing powers as legitimate.

Then, in one of those peculiarly Alaskan happenings, the state legislature met in special session and declared a limit to the land tax that the new North Slope Borough could impose. "Absolutely discriminatory legislation," Mr. Hopson told me, "that removed from the borough a substantial part of its tax base. The legislature put stiff requirements and limitations on our ability to tax."

The forces which have changed Barrow's economic and political structure have also affected some of the traditional Eskimo ways. On a lovely spring day—only ten below and no wind—I walked along the shore of the Arctic Ocean and watched children playing out on the ice. It was the kind of day on which men talk of whaling, as the sun lifts cautiously over the horizon and rides along low in the sky, promising soon to come and stay.

Tommy Brower, a spare man with kind eyes and a gentle disposition, still takes a boat out in the spring, aging as slowly, it seems, as a pine on a windswept mountain. But he senses a different mood, a change that has come with these modern times.

"It seems to be every man for himself these days," he told me. "These young fellows go out there in the boats and chase the whale this way and that, too far out into the deep water and the heavy ice. If their boat makes the kill, they have a hard time bringing it in. Then, they expect everyone to come and help, which is the way it's supposed to be from the beginning."

THE VILLAGE OF KAKTOVIK, on Barter Island, is surely one of the loneliest in the Arctic. Yet, such are the peculiar tides of human activity in the Arctic that the island was once a place of activity and assembly. In prehistoric times, it was a stop on the trade route that ran westward from Canada. Each summer people of the Thule culture of the Arctic camped there and bartered goods on their way to a great fair held at the mouth of the Colville River, 175 miles west.

The village has traditionally subsisted on a large caribou herd that migrates there in the spring and on marine mammals in the Arctic Ocean. The age of atomic weapons has brought change. When the Distant Early Warning system was constructed in the early 1950's, Kaktovik found itself thrust into the heart of the 20th century; the island became a DEW station.

Today, the most prominent features of the landscape for many hundreds of miles around are two white plastic radar dishes and a pair of communications scoops that look like wolf ears. The base occupies the north end of the flat island, while the small village sits on a protected bay a half mile to the east. In the immense whiteness of winter, Barter Island seemed to be a gray erasure mark on a piece of fine bond paper. It had looked that way for two years prior to my visit in 1975, for the ice of the Beaufort Sea never went out during that time, and the island had been locked in its grip for many, many long months.

Marx Sims—a young man from Kansas who is mayor, postmaster, school board member, and airline station manager—came down to the airstrip to pick me up in a new truck. He had first come to the island as a civilian employee under contract with the Air Force; he married a local Eskimo girl, settled on the island, and then was drafted into the Army. After his discharge, he returned to Kaktovik, and a different world.

We sat in Marx's comfortable house drinking coffee; his corner desk was littered with papers and documents.

"With the land-claims act, a new government, and oil development,

Supply sled in tow, an Eskimo speeds across tundra to hunt caribou. Snow-mobiles have greater range than dogsleds, once the only means of winter travel.

we are losing a way of life that was a good one," he said. "But we are getting something in exchange—a chance to have the kids educated in the home village, to keep their roots here. For a lot of Eskimo young people, being uprooted and displaced has only meant trouble with drink and drugs, and for some of them, it is already too late."

There are about a dozen surnames in this village of 138 people, and, as so often occurs along this old whaling coast, the names reflect the heritage of 19th-century whalers from New England: Brower, Gordon, Rexford.

More than most, perhaps, the people of Kaktovik have a stake in the success of the borough government at Barrow. The DEW station may close someday, and a proposed gas pipeline to Canada may be routed the other way—south from Prudhoe Bay instead of east past Kaktovik. In that event, the borough government will become the economic mainstay.

"Now that the borough can tax the oil companies," Marx said, "that could save the north. But this whole situation is full of frustrations, hopes, pitfalls, and promises." He picked up a handful of papers and held them out. "Staying alive here is a full-time job, but I have to take time from getting water and wood to fill out revenue-sharing forms!"

At this point, the frustrations seem to be outnumbering the hopes. The borough's capital-improvement program has built only a one-lane road rather than the promised two-lane road. And, although every village was promised a school by the borough, the one at Kaktovik was never finished. The Bureau of Indian Affairs and the State of Alaska, having turned over the school to the Natives, take no further responsibility in the matter of education. Kaktovik's children have been left hanging.

The mainland across from Barter Island is still one of the world's most prolific caribou calving grounds; usually as many as 120,000 animals of the

Porcupine herd, after wintering in Canada, wander just a few miles from the village in early summer. Largely to protect that herd and its migration route, the Arctic National Wildlife Range was established in 1960. With nearly nine million acres and a proposed addition of more than three million, this largest of all such ranges sprawls across one of the emptiest and most stupefyingly magnificent stretches of land on earth.

Ave Thayer, the range manager, is a spare, direct man. Yet he can speak poetry about the range, and I discovered why when we made a long flight into the far eastern Arctic. We flew north from Fairbanks over frozen foothills, banked over the mountains, then dropped into the long valley of the Hulahula River, between two of the highest peaks in the Brooks Range —9,020-foot Mount Chamberlin and 8,855-foot Mount Michelson.

Scoured, sanded, and planed by glaciers, softened by a mantle of snow, glazed with ice, polished by storms of only imagined violence and intensity, and illuminated by gleaming sunlight, these peaks of the eastern Brooks Range became to me a boundless, free-form sculpture. Our fragile aircraft made only a small buzz in that expanse of wilderness as it circled back up the Kongakut, a deep narrow valley that cuts far into the mountains. The willow-lined streambed was stitched with moose tracks, and the great animals themselves were scattered throughout the valley.

Topping a pass, hazy with blown snow, we turned down the watershed of the Sheenjek. It gradually widened into a truly monumental valley, miles wide, flat, and rimmed with handsome mountains; we landed on a long, narrow lake. I stepped out, put on my snowshoes, and instantly toppled off them, sinking deep into loose snow. The caribou, with more sense, were feeding quietly on a plateau beyond a small rise at the shore. We mushed up the rise and stood for a moment watching the utterly peaceful scene, in a land never developed, hardly ever coveted, and certainly never abused by man. In all of that vast world, under a sky of total blue, there was not a single sound.

"The sense of what the Arctic is," said Ave, "comes to you after you've spent a week camped in a place like this. You become very aware of the sound of birds flying, animals moving. These stimuli are subtle, and the eyes and ears become very sensitive to even slight signals. You notice the tiny trace of a shrew —just a few millimeters long—that crosses your snowshoe tracks. You pick up a bird's feather, and you find yourself examining its architecture for a long time. But then, when you get back to Fairbanks, the sensitivity that equipped you well for the Arctic has to be turned way down or the amount and level of noise and activity will overwhelm you. I know people who can even screen out fire engines."

LIKE SO MANY OTHER ALASKAN TOWNS, Nome came into existence in an improbable place because of human greed, fortitude, desperation, and luck. Its very name is said to have backed into history. A cartographer in the hydrographic office of Britain's Royal Navy, pondering this bulge on the southern coast of Seward Peninsula, made a notation next to it: "Name?" Through a later engraver's mistake it became Cape Nome, and Nome became history in September 1898, when a man named Lindeberg "hit pay" along Anvil Creek.

When word finally flew out across Alaska, a ragtag army of hopeful gold seekers descended upon the area. Then, in 1900, more arrivals from the rest of the United States transformed the village into a sprawling town. For nearly a decade there existed a life of such rawness that the sounds of the brawls, busts, bars, and brothels still echo in legend.

Few rougher, tougher towns than Nome ever were. First populated by the gaunt remnant of those who made the long trek over the Chilkoot Pass and down the Yukon, then joined by eager youngsters fresh from the West Coast and by curious Eskimos drawn to town by the promise of grub, liquor, and excitement, Nome swelled to 3,000 people by 1899. In the midst of this spectacle, the absolutely improbable happened. A sourdough shut out from the creek claims, and given to that peculiar urge that makes men seek gold in any speck of dust located at any place, began listlessly panning outside his tent pitched on the beach one day when he was sick. He found the precious stuff right there in the black-ruby sand.

Soon the beach was crawling with miners, a teeming hive of fortune seekers who settled on the unwritten rule that a person could prospect as much sand as he could dig with a shovel. And, in an act of symbolic power, nature wiped the slate clean with every tide.

By the end of summer 1900, Nome resembled a huge shipwreck washed ashore; 20,000 men churned the mud of Front Street into a mire. Saloons, gambling dens, and houses of ill repute flourished, and characters of sufficient proportion soon appeared to give the place the proper style — men like Wyatt Earp, who came up from the American West with a reputation as marshal and gunslinger. He became co-owner of one of Nome's most notorious saloons.

But gradually both the population and the amount of gold dwindled. In 1913 a furious storm blew Nome to pieces, driving schooners through town and out onto the tundra and splintering houses like matchboxes. In the violent wind and dark, Nome's pretentions to urbanity vanished.

But Nome, reduced to just 2,600 people, kept going as a supply base for gold-seeking ventures in Siberia, as a trading center for furs, ivories, and skins, and as a gold center. It lived on in the shadow of its rich past until 1971, when the land-claims settlement brought a new bonanza of money and hope.

Nome was still deep in winter when I arrived there; a storm had piled water up the Snake River, and a hard cold had frozen it there, several feet higher than the bridge into town. A high wind was blowing the snow down Front Street, and the prospect was so forlorn that it was hard to credit history and imagine a narrow, crowded street in 1900 lined with board buildings and teeming with thousands of miners.

In Nome, I met a crusty, hard-nosed old miner who, to me, was cast from the same mold as the roughhewn stampeders of the past. He has lived in Alaska since 1932 and has worked a mining claim about 15 miles out of town for 37 years. He has been a bird of passage most of his life, having left home at 13 to hire on to the last of the working sailing ships. When the Depression came, he borrowed two bits from his boss and tossed it in the air: "Heads, Fairbanks; tails, Nome!"

"It came tails, and here I am," he said. He looks the part of a gold miner

—his Nordic features weathered by age and hard work, but his eyes still young. "Work?" he said, and he leaned on the word as though it were a talisman. "These guys walking around, what do they know about hard work? My sons and I have a dredge over on our claim. To get it there, we took it apart and packed it over the mountain by sled—fifty trips. Then I built a steam locomotive."

"A locomotive?" I asked with astonishment.

"Sure. Took the pieces in and put it together. *Hard work.* And what do I have to show for all these years of such work? Nothing!" He put his head back and laughed the laugh of the just.

"These young people today," he resumed, "they come to Nome and fall into these liquor holes. If they would carry a dredge over a mountain and put it together in the cold we have up here, they would soon find out what it is all about. But no, they sit in the liquor holes and live on the welfare checks. And now people in town tell me that I might have to buy these claims I've worked for 37 years."

This old miner not only has small regard for those who receive "something for nothing" through the welfare system, but also a grievance, justified or not, against the perpetrators of the Alaska Native Claims Settlement Act. He thinks he may have to register the claims he has worked all these years and have them formally patented and conveyed to him. The surveys are running as much as a thousand dollars per claim, and he has six claims.

Anticipating these expenses, he has found more gold for less work in the tourists who visit Nome in the summer, and who, for some reason that puzzles him, will pay to visit him and see what he has done in this hard, remote country.

"I talk to them," he said. "They are lonely people. They are sad people. They think they will be happier by seeing something. That is all a dream of theirs, but I talk to them anyway."

He ponders the surface of his coffee, makes a half-submerged sound in his throat, and slowly shakes his head. "It isn't the tourists. They are only sad. It is the politicians who kill the world. Now they want to make a desert out of Alaska. After all the hard work put into this state they want to make a desert out of it. I will tell you the end of it. We bought Alaska for $7,200,000 once, then we bought it again for a billion, and in the end we are all going to lose it."

I wondered about that. I remembered once being at a high pass, the slopes burnished by winds of awesome velocity. And just as I had decided that no living thing could possibly survive in such a place, there was a flutter of small white wings and a flock of ptarmigan started into the clean air.

Perhaps there is nothing stronger or safer than a feather in a gale.

Ramshackle hulk of the Donaldson *weathers in the sand and backwater of a Nome beach. From the late 1920's, the diesel-powered freighter plied the waters of the Bering Sea, bringing mail and supplies to coastal towns. Then, in 1945, one of the Arctic's raging storms wrenched the boat from its mooring and cast it far up on the shore. Today, only airplanes serve these communities.*

ENTHEOS

6/Alaska: The Northern Giant

MARCH IS STILL FULL WINTER IN ALASKA, but dreams of summer begin to stir, and the restless spirit, cabined in for many months, seeks some outward sign of a promised change. On the frozen Tanana River, 60 miles west of Fairbanks, a tripod is set up, connected by a cord to a timepiece. Participants in a public lottery guess the exact moment when the ice will begin to thaw and move downstream under the influence of the warming sun. That first movement of the ice trips the clock, and by this arbitrary measure, "break up" begins in Alaska.

The lottery winners, and there are often many, receive several thousand dollars apiece, but it is in the lift to the entire state's morale that break up is hailed as a critical event—even though it issues in a time of mud, slush, flood, and disorder.

No man knows for certain when old Alaska and its "Last Frontier" society began to break up, when the glacial forces of world energy needs, rights of Native populations, desire to preserve wilderness and to protect unique animal populations, began to move and shift, but there are several popular candidates.

For most people, July 18, 1968, is a natural. On that day oil gushed from an exploration well listed as Prudhoe Bay State No. 1, the 51st hole —and the final one planned—that had been punched into the North Slope since 1944. This last throw of the dice by British Petroleum and its partner, Atlantic Richfield Corporation, paid off. In September 1969, the State of Alaska sold off oil leases and made 900 million dollars in a single morning. Once again "North to the Future" became the slogan of a genuine boom.

Other observers think that break up began on that emotional day, January 3, 1959, when Sourdough Alaska threw its crumpled hat into the air in joy at becoming the 49th State. One of its most optimistic, and misguided, expectations was that it would now be free of the constraints of the Federal Government, which had been its landlord—and its generous patron—for so many years.

Under terms of the Statehood Act, Alaska had the right to select 103.5 million acres of land from a public domain of 375 million. The purposes, then, seemed quite clear: economic development and the building of a local economy to get the state off the federal dole. Alaska began to gather in land, minerals, timber, and other resources with the intention of transferring them into private hands for development.

But by 1962, only 30 percent of the state's land had been patented, and the rest was unavailable for any purpose since the federal Bureau of Land

Fired by the Arctic sun, ice fog eddies past drilling rigs and a section of the trans-Alaska pipeline (foreground) near Prudhoe Bay. "Ever closer . . . swirl forces which will change this land forever," said Governor Jay S. Hammond. Oil development—with its associated demands on housing, social services, and the environment—has a major impact on Alaska's life and land.

Comes of Age

By Joseph Judge

Management was requiring several years to make land conveyances. The state consoled itself, however, with the notion that it still had 22 years remaining in which to pick up the rest of its land as it continued to grow and develop. Besides, most of the land that was worthwhile—including the oil field at Prudhoe Bay—was already under the flag with the Big Dipper and the North Star.

A third candidate for the break up of old Alaska is that day in 1960 when John Nusunginya was arrested for shooting eider ducks. An international treaty controlling the hunting of migratory birds had been entered into by great and distant governments—and reaffirmed by the State of Alaska in 1959. But John and his fellow Eskimos of the North Slope had always shot ducks for food without regard to season. Two days after John's arrest, 138 men showed up to hunt ducks illegally, and to make the point that some consideration should be given to people who had a historic claim to the land before laws were passed governing its use.

A few months earlier, the U. S. Atomic Energy Commission in faraway Washington, D. C., had announced a scheme, called Project Chariot, to create a harbor on the shore of harborless Cape Thompson, near the Eskimo village of Point Hope, by blowing a huge hole in the shore with an atomic bomb. Eskimo artist Howard Rock said at the time: "They did not make a tiny effort to consult the Natives who lived close by."

After all, who owned Alaska?

ALL OVER THE STATE Native organizations sprang up in response to the fact that neither the Alaska purchase nor the Statehood Act had established the rights of the Indians, Eskimos, and Aleuts to the land they had occupied for untold centuries.

Willie Hensley, the darkly handsome and brilliant Eskimo political leader, recalled for me that pivotal period: "The State of Alaska, faced with potential bankruptcy, wanted to push ahead with the oil exploration and land selections. At the same time, the oil companies wanted to verify that their leases were legal, and to build the trans-Alaska pipeline. And we were confident; we had no idea of failure. We had never been defeated by the U. S. Cavalry."

The question of land ownership had been squarely put, and until he got an answer from Congress, then Secretary of the Interior Stewart L. Udall, who administered much of the state, did a remarkably courageous—or outrageous—thing. He halted the transfer of both federal land and oil and gas leases until the Native claims had been settled.

The land freeze remained in force until passage of the Alaska Native Claims Settlement Act in 1971. That act is one of the most remarkable—and least understood—pieces of legislation ever passed by a democratic government. In a way it absolves the American conscience of more than 300 years of broken treaties with Native Americans.

But it does much more. It makes capitalists out of the descendants of the aboriginal occupants of the state by placing most of their forty million acres in Native-owned-and-administered, profit-making corporations. These large corporations are underwritten with one billion dollars in payments for rights and claims.

The land-claims settlement, the establishment of the corporations, the recognition by Natives that they are shareholders, has contributed to a resurgence of Native pride that is stirring new life from the ashes of neglect and welfare and alcoholism. It is one of the most powerful forces in modern Alaskan life. The white citizens of the state, the vast majority comfortably housed in the urban centers of Anchorage, Fairbanks, and Juneau, are apt to judge the young Native from the caricature seen staggering from the bars of Second Street in Fairbanks or Fourth Avenue in Anchorage—a caricature that is sunk in liquor and blind violence. And it is true that the end is not yet, that a generation still hangs in the balance.

Yet the social change and the struggle to obtain fair legislation and fair treatment have already brought to the fore a cadre of Native political and social leaders as impressive as any this nation has produced—John Sackett of Galena; Willie Hensley and John Ward Schaeffer, Jr., of Kotzebue; Eben Hopson and Joe Upicksoun of Barrow; Phillip Guy and Emil Notti of Bethel; John Borbridge of Juneau, to mention only a few.

One Native leader told me: "I spent ten years of my life drinking, in despair, not knowing what culture I belonged to. I have a special relationship to my community. I understand the dilemma. But I know we will find the right way by going back to the old ways of group decision and community and pride in self."

Another has a motto over his desk: "I dream of what can be, and ask 'why not?'"

Sackett is a state senator. Hensley ran a strong race for the U. S. House in 1974 before losing. Hopson has formed a borough government on the North Slope and in 1976 won the Democratic nomination for Alaska's single Con-

Rebekah Kolmetz Metcalf directs pipeline construction traffic in Valdez. With her savings, she plans to return to Florida and raise tomatoes.

gressional seat. All of these men seem intent on employing the wealth of their corporations to protect and sustain the traditional life of their people.

A volatile by-product of this effort is a subtle change just under the surface of Alaskan life in the long-standing amity that has existed between the whites and their Native companions of the former frontier. In the past, racial intolerance and discrimination were never pronounced in a country so large, with such a small population following similar life-styles.

With the enfranchisement of the Native as an economic citizen and the growth of racial pride, however, intolerance of whites and a resentment of past treatment has become something of a cachet among some typically rebellious young. This is especially true in the halfway houses like Barrow, Kotzebue, Bethel, and Fort Yukon. These are neither traditional Native communities nor white men's cities, but simply collections of services, like schools and hospitals; here, the young find neither the security of the village nor the opportunity of the city.

One longtime hunter and guide told me, "When the day comes, when a Native kicks me off land I've been hunting for 20 years, that day blood will start to run."

But the public domain—where hunting was almost always free—has been reduced in size, and as the complicated processes of transfer of land titles continue to carve up the state into smaller and smaller units, each man will have to find his own place—just as he has in the Lower Forty-Eight. The important point for the moment is that the Native will have a place, and it is not on a reservation.

AS ALASKAN SOCIETY UNDERGOES ALTERATION, symbolic figures emerge to represent the powerful interests at work. To me, Sandy Hamilton is one such figure. A red-bearded refugee from the physical and emotional smog of the Outside, Sandy married a lovely Eskimo girl and built a cabin in the village of Allakaket, along the Koyukuk River. He knows how to run dogs, how to fly a bush plane, how to hunt to put meat on the table. He accepts the land on its own terms. He also knows what he wants from life. And what he wants and what people on the Outside want from Alaska may be mutually exclusive.

I chatted with Sandy one day in Anaktuvuk Pass, a community deep in the heart of the Brooks Range.

He was surprised at the capricious way that many people behave in Alaska. "I've heard about pipeline workers building a dozen trails across the tundra where only one would be sufficient. And there's a story about some clowns turning on a tractor, pointing it north, and just letting it go its merry way."

He shook his head with sad—and confused—resignation. "In this place, you learn to save and use everything that's important, or you don't live. At least not for long."

The Alaskan bush conceals many Sandy Hamiltons. To a man they regard the wisdom of wind and weather, of accommodation to superior natural forces, as the key to survival. Thus they are surprised, and even repelled, by the corporate attitude—to defeat the environment, to march to the North Slope and build a moon base with a swimming pool and a tree —which they regard as essentially colonial, implying the power of a transplanted culture.

And they follow the equation to its end. The exertion of mastery over the harshest of environments is impressive, but the waste and cost are outrageous, and the end products are greater pollution in decaying cities, the continued proliferation of automobiles and plastic, and the social inequality of suburbs.

"What happens," Sandy asks, "when the Eskimo who earns $20 an hour on the pipeline finds himself back in his village hunting caribou? In the end he's the one who will pay the emotional cost so that a New Yorker can watch color television."

These remarks were made at a time before it became clear that—final and bitterest of ironies—New York probably would receive no Alaskan oil, or Chicago either. It became clear, after seven years of court struggles, ever-escalating cost, and violent social upheaval, that there exists no practical means of refining the Alaskan oil, and transporting it from West Coast ports to the Midwest and East, where it is most needed.

"That is why the Japanese buyers are so often pictured smiling," said an unsmiling friend of mine. "Certainly the big oil companies must have known from the very beginning that Prudhoe Bay is all dressed up with no place to go."

IN MARCH OF 1976, the Fairbanks *Daily News Miner* announced that its annual special "Progress Edition," published for 26 years, would henceforth be eliminated. There had been progress quite enough; a lot of people think progress too much.

My friend Fabian Carey would have agreed with that. When he died unexpectedly in the autumn of 1975, a lot of old Alaska seemed to go with him in my mind.

For the better part of 30 years, Fabian had trapped for marten along the Kuskokwim River and in the alpine country on the northwest slope of Mount McKinley, around Lake Minchumina. I first met him on a stingingly cold winter day at the International Bar in Fairbanks. He had just been elected head of a new organization, the Alaska Trappers Association.

"We finally decided we had better organize," he told me, "although a man living his life in the woods is not too good at that. Sometimes you've got to knock these fellows down to make them listen."

He stood at the window and looked out at the clinging ice fog; every branch of every tree was covered with a white coating.

"I see what's happening in this state, and it's like watching a storm coming," Fabian said with a deep sigh. "First the Statehood Act, then this oil push. When I think of the cruelties that have been visited upon Alaska! This land-claims business is just to get the Natives out of the government's hair while the oil is tapped, but Natives here have been citizens for more than 50 years.

"What is happening here amounts to entombment of the land, between the Federal Government taking what it wants and the Natives taking what they want. It's happened before, Outside, and the result is that freedom tends to vanish."

Fabian had more than a practical interest in his profession. His bedroom was filled with memorabilia of early trapping days—letters and pages from diaries kept by old trappers whose names he knew, as well as where their lines ran.

Fabian's career as a trapper began at age 19 the hard way. He became partners with an older, experienced trapper.

"For eight months, I saw exactly *(Continued on page 180)*

173

"Roughnecks," part of a 25,000-man oil-related work force in Alaska, sink drill pipe at one of the 150 wells that will tap the oil reserves at Prudhoe Bay. Drawn to bleak Arctic slopes by huge salaries, pipeline crews work as many as eight weeks of grueling 12-hour days, then fly out to visit families or to squander wages in such places as Fairbanks' bustling bar district (upper, left).

At the southern end of the pipeline, in Valdez, a welder in a bar succumbs to fatigue. Along with population growth and an inflated economy, have come serious human problems—crime, split families, and alcoholism. Many Alaskans, like Governor Hammond, wonder if oil forms a "windfall spilled from God's grand cornucopia or simply crawled from Pandora's box."

ALL BY NATIONAL GEOGRAPHIC PHOTOGRAPHER STEVE RAYMER

Demolished by an earthquake in 1964, Valdez faces new tremors from the oil boom: housing shortages, overburdened utilities, and expensive supplies. The population of Valdez—once a small fishing village—has skyrocketed 600 percent to 7,000 people in just four years. Pipeline workers pay as much as $1,000 a month to rent mobile homes (above, center); others live for less in dormitories. Valdez residents call the changes in their town "exciting and fascinating, but also upsetting and uncomfortable." At Keystone Canyon near Valdez, welders (left) join 2,500-foot-long sections of steel pipe. Storage tanks (above, right) creep up slopes in front of Mount Kate south of Valdez. Built on bedrock in an effort to prevent oil spills caused by earthquakes, the tanks hold as much as a million barrels of oil each. A floating derrick sinks pilings for one of the four docks that will berth oil supertankers.

Twenty-two-wheel truck rolls north on the haul road through Atigun Pass in the Brooks Range, transporting a 153-foot-long bridge beam. Drivers of rigs like this one belong to Teamsters Union Local 959. A growing power in the 49th State, Local 959 has 23,000 members from some 80 different occupations—oil workers, telephone operators, policemen, butchers, and bakers. The union has a huge pension and welfare fund—financed almost entirely by the members' employers—which grows by a million dollars a week. Jesse L. Carr (right), head of Alaska's Teamsters, stands outside the union's 20-million-dollar combination hospital, office complex, and recreation center in Anchorage. About the state's future, he says, "Jobs is what it's all about." An ardent supporter of Alaska's development, Carr has asserted, "You're not going to stop the growth of this state!"

one Indian and one partner. Then I snowshoed 75 miles into town. When I got back, my partner had made off with the furs and the gun, and I had three dollars to show for eight months in the woods. I learned the truth of it—trapping is a lone-wolf game."

Fabian had an invisible enemy, whose presence you can sense, because you, yourself, are a part of that enemy's army: "Massman," Fabian called him.

He had a long list of things that Massman could not understand, but the central one was that the acquisition of things is meaningless, even demeaning, to human life.

"I see those tourists coming up here in the summer," he said, "grabbing up old kerosene lamps and sleigh bells, the junk of the last generation —but what stands up is the paper and the ideas that are written down on it. Let me tell you, we suffer. We suffer because Massman can't get it through his head that no one really, ever, *owns* anything. We only use things for the little time we are here. The only thing a man owns is his life."

As we talked that day, a middle-aged woman came into the bar and said to Fabian, "You still running around in the woods?"

"Well," he said with a shrug, "after being up here so long there's not much point in leaving."

"Hell," she said, "I forgot what I came up here for."

WITH THE DISCOVERY OF OIL, then, came the promise of wealth. With the land-claims act came a new sense of future and pride for the Alaskan Native. With it also came a chance to set aside vast acreages for public purposes other than development.

In exchange for their compliance in pushing through the land-claims act, conservationists won a provision that authorized the Secretary of the Interior to withdraw as much as 80 million acres from the public domain for possible inclusion in the "four systems"—new national parks, forests, wildlife refuges, and wild and scenic rivers.

The scale and scope of some of the government's four-systems recommendations—which later totaled 83 million acres—staggered many Alaskans. Among the highlights:

—Three massive new national parks: Gates of the Arctic, 8.4 million acres; Wrangell-St. Elias, 8.6 million acres; Lake Clark, 2.6 million acres.

—Four new national monuments: Aniakchak Caldera, Harding Icefield-Kenai Fiords, Cape Krusenstern, and Kobuk Valley—adding up to almost 3 million acres.

—Additions to existing federal reserves: more than 3 million acres to Mount McKinley National Park, and almost 2 million acres to Katmai National Monument.

—Addition of more than 31 million acres to the National Wildlife Refuge System, including a large supplement to the existing Arctic National Wildlife Range in the eastern Brooks Range; and the establishment of these new refuges: 3.6 million acres in the Yukon Flats, 7.6 million acres centered on the Noatak River basin, more than 5 million acres in the Yukon Delta, and more than 4 million acres along the Koyukuk, Yukon, and Innoko Rivers.

—More than 18 million acres of new national forest, the Yukon-Kuskokwim area being the largest, with significant tracts set aside along the Porcupine River and in the Wrangell Mountains.

—Twenty wild rivers scattered throughout the state.

Dr. Robert Weeden, director of Alaska's Policy Development and Planning agency until 1976, told me in his Juneau office: "The question before Alaska, to my mind, is what kind of society do we want to build here? Do we want what they have Outside, an industrialized society that makes maximum use of its salable resources, or a different, more stable and more comfortable society interacting with our splendid environment?"

When conservation groups had the proposed pipeline tied in a legal knot, those Alaskans who felt they were being denied their birthright displayed bumper stickers reading "Sierra Club Go Home," or "Alaska for Alaskans," or even "Independence for Alaska."

Now the stickers read "Happiness Is 10,000 Okies Going Home With a Texan Under Each Arm." Everyone knew the pipeline was coming, that it would be something like the Normandy Beach landing.

But no one was ready for the reality of it all—the flood of big money as everyone began pulling down big salaries, the housing shortage, the increase in crime, the powerful social impact on small communities like Valdez.

In Alaska, life has always been lived in the presence of the overriding fact that one is at the end of the line: the tenuous supply line that runs risk and cost up through the roof, that makes luxuries of things people take for granted Outside, and that preserves for Alaska the economic posture it has always had—that of a colony.

Conservationists in Anchorage protest the leasing of offshore oil and gas rights in the Gulf of Alaska. The 1976 sale, also opposed by the State, earned 572 million dollars for the Federal Government.

Men have come to Alaska to take the raw materials out, to create wealth elsewhere. When the Guggenheims and the Morgans went after the copper deposit at Kennicott in the Wrangells, they built a steamship company, a railroad, and a town. When the immense copper deposit was played out, so was the rest of it.

It has always been thus. The millions of dollars worth of furs and skins went off to St. Petersburg or San Francisco (Continued on page 186)

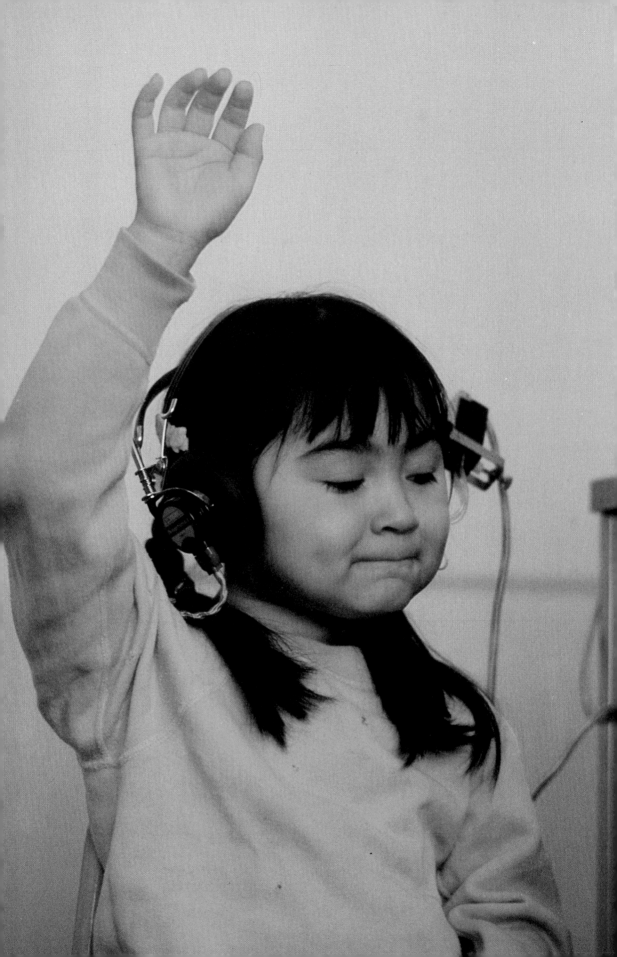

NATIONAL GEOGRAPHIC PHOTOGRAPHER BRUCE DALE (ABOVE)

Corporation stockholder (left), one of the youngest under the Alaska Native Claims Settlement Act, takes a hearing test before entering school at Gambell on St. Lawrence Island. More than 75,000 Native Alaskans born before passage of the act on December 18, 1971, have registered for shares in village and regional corporations—managers of land and money granted by the Federal Government. Such controlled use of their wealth confused many Natives; television broadcasts like the one above explained the workings of the law. After 1976, stockholders will share the dividends their corporations earn; until then, they receive only small cash payments. Passage of the act climaxed ten years of a highly organized effort spearheaded by Natives like Eben Hopson (below), an Eskimo leader in Barrow.

"*The unique recreational value of Alaska lies in its frontier character," U. S. Forest Service explorer Robert Marshall wrote in 1938. Today, a wish to find a "new land large enough to breathe in and expand the spirit," as Governor Hammond says, still draws many people, like the hitchhiker (above) lounging beside the road near Mount McKinley National Park. Like other large national parks, McKinley feels the burden of too many people in too small an area. Bumper-to-bumper traffic on the Kenai Peninsula moves homeward to Anchorage at the end of a July weekend. Many Alaskans wonder if overcrowding will bring the same problems found in the Lower Forty-Eight.*

or Seattle. The millions of dollars worth of whale oil and baleen went off to New England and California, and what was left behind was a diseased and demoralized Native minority. Little of the wealth wrested from Alaska over the centuries has stayed there.

Now many fear that history will repeat itself with the pipeline — the huge salaries will be drained off to Texas and Oklahoma, the profits to Houston and New York and Geneva and the tax-free Cayman Islands, and Alaska will be left with the bill for broken roads, unused schools, and wide-ranging social services.

That is why, when a bleached-blonde waitress at the Fairbanks airport bar says to a departing Cowboy Hat, "You bring me back a jar of that Texas dirt, 'cause I want to just play in it real deep!" the old-time Alaskan puts down his half-finished beer and leaves the bar.

The problem Alaska faces, of course, is that there is not another choice of an economy. In this respect, the 49th State is closer to the countries of the Third World than it is to its own parent nation. It can exploit the exploiters, or starve.

One Alaskan told me, "Getting the oil out is a matter of national priority, or so we are told. Then why should Alaskans pay for the damage done in meeting that priority? Why, for example, should our highway system be broken down so someone somewhere else can enjoy air conditioning and drip-dry clothing?"

To which the bankers retort: "Without our risk money, the state would go back to being a howling wilderness."

To which the conservationists reply: "Great!"

MEANWHILE, most of those living through this transition period want things both ways. Villagers would like to hold onto their subsistence style of life — but also maintain the welfare, food stamps, snow machines, and mail planes. Many young people would rather visit a bar than a trapline. And even the most ardent developer feels a pang when he sees a part of the great wilderness bisected by a road. And those social workers, journalists, and consultants who frequently travel the bush still rejoice at the convenience of having a good dinner, a soft bed, and a warm bath in a modern Anchorage hotel.

Will we have the best of both worlds, or soon be on the road to the worst of both? Can we have all of Alaska's myriad treasures, including the esthetic, or will we end up with none at all? Which way will the transition fall out? After the pipeline — what?

One day I flew far into the far north range, up the valley of the Coleen River, to a place as remote from man's marks as any on this earth. A mountain vastness filled my vision to its limits in every direction. The ground below was laced with countless animal tracks.

We landed on a small lake and snowshoed to the crest of a gentle hill. From this vantage, we watched a herd of caribou quietly grazing through the snow cover. Silence. Silence and beauty and a world balanced between life and death. One could feel the equilibrium of nature, its awesome, planetary scale, pursuing a destiny and harboring a great secret we could not fathom.

Caribou antler juts from autumn-tinged tundra
in the Brooks Range. Such pristine lands pose a
dilemma for Alaska: how to balance the
development of natural resources with the
preservation of untrammeled wilderness.

*T*wilight colors Mount Sanford in the proposed Wrangell-St. Elias National Park. Conservationists

and miners heatedly debate whether the park should include adjacent mineral-rich lands.

GALEN ROWELL (LEFT); A. DURAND JONES

Gleaming ramparts of Mount McKinley, called *Denali* —the Great One—by Athapascan Indians, soar above their image in Reflection Pond. Only this northern half of the peak lies within the national park. A proposed addition at the southern side of the park would include the rest of the mountain—as well as the granite bastions of Cathedral Spires (above). The extension would also protect critical habitats for caribou, sheep, moose, and wolves. Eighty-three million acres of proposed national parks, forests, wild rivers, and wildlife refuges contribute to the controversy over the destiny of Alaska's land. Conservationists and the Federal Government want the land protected by such federal preserves; many Alaskans advocate state control over much of these lands; economic interests want them available for private ownership and development. By 1978, Congress hopes to unravel the tangle of ideals and claims, and determine the future of Alaska's wilderness.

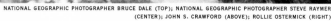

*A*ntlers haloed by a fading autumn sun, caribou in the Arctic graze during a migration to winter range. In Alaska, a land of short summers and fragile environments, animals like the caribou often need enormous areas for survival. With development of the state, man and his machines have encroached increasingly on the habitats of Alaska's wildlife. A brown bear (left) feasts on a sockeye salmon in Katmai National Monument. A bull moose, its antlers a choice trophy for hunters, walks through autumn snow in the forests of the Kenai Peninsula. In winter white, an Arctic fox lopes after its prey near Prudhoe Bay. A mottled eggshell at Tebay Lakes marks a new generation of ptarmigan. A proposed 31.6-million-acre addition to Alaska's wildlife refuges will double the acreage already protected in the United States and help preserve the state's wild creatures.

*S*inuous gravel ridges, created by winds and waves over thousands of years, form Cape Krusenstern, curving into the Chukchi Sea on Alaska's northwest coast. Some 5,000 years ago, Eskimo peoples camped and hunted on the first ridge of this beachline. Today, the 114 ridges of Cape Krusenstern provide a record — through tools, weapons, and remains of houses — of at least ten distinct phases of Eskimo cultural development. Eighty-year-old Edna Williams (below), whose Inupiaq Eskimo name, Napaaktuk, means tree — an anomaly along this treeless coast — prepares a dish from the intestines of a bearded seal, or *oogruk*. Her people still hunt sea mammals from the cape. The proposed Cape Krusenstern National Monument, where Edna's people will continue subsistence hunting, fishing, and gathering of wild plants as they have for millenniums, will preserve a part of Alaska's wild, free heritage — a heritage of both land and people.

AUTHORS' NOTES

INDEX

Boldface indicates illustrations;
italic refers to picture captions

Managing Editor **William R. Gray**, a native of Washington, D. C., joined the Special Publications staff as a writer in 1968 after graduating from Bucknell University. A veteran backpacker, Will hiked from Mexico to Canada for the Special Publication *The Pacific Crest Trail* and climbed the highest peak in Yugoslavia for *The Alps*.

Before coming to the National Geographic in 1969, **Noel Grove** worked as a railroad section hand, a farm laborer, a construction worker, and a high school English teacher. He has written articles for NATIONAL GEOGRAPHIC on wheat harvesters, the bicycle boom, oil, Mark Twain, Venezuela, and volcanoes in Iceland.

Joseph Judge, Senior Assistant Editor in charge of articles for NATIONAL GEOGRAPHIC, has journeyed to Alaska five times. During his 13-year career with the Society, Joe has written about Hong Kong, Israel, Venice, New Orleans, Boston, Central Florida, the Grand Canyon, the Wind River Mountains, and the Zulus of Africa.

A staff writer for NATIONAL GEOGRAPHIC since 1972, **Fred Kline** has reported on Baltimore, the Library of Congress, and his hometown of San Antonio. Previously, he taught English at Columbus College of Art and Design in Ohio. He received a master's degree in creative writing from San Francisco State University, and has published four books of poetry.

Managing Editor of National Geographic Books for Young Explorers, **Cynthia Russ Ramsay** first visited Alaska for the Special Publication *Life in Rural America*. Earlier, she traveled among the mountains of Austria for *The Alps*. Cynthia, a native of New York City and a graduate of Hunter College, joined the Society's staff in 1966.

197

ACKNOWLEDGMENTS

The Special Publications Division is grateful to the individuals, organizations, and agencies named or quoted in the text and to those cited here for their generous cooperation and assistance during the preparation of this book: Judith E. Ayres, Earl Bartlett, George Herben, Neil and Elizabeth Johannsen, A. Durand Jones, Marcy Jones, James Pepper, William C. Reffalt, and Pete Robinson; Alaska Division of State Libraries and Museums, Alaska Division of Tourism, Embassy of Canada, Fairbanks Impact Information Center, National Park Service, the Office of the Governor of Alaska, Smithsonian Institution, University of Alaska, University of Washington, U. S. Forest Service, Yukon Archives, and the Yukon Territory Department of Tourism & Information.

ADDITIONAL READING

Robert D. Arnold, *Alaska Native Land Claims;* Hector Chevigny, *Russian America;* Merle Colby, *A Guide to Alaska: Last American Frontier;* Bryan Cooper, *The Last Frontier;* Philip H. Godsell, *The Romance of the Alaska Highway;* Ernest Gruening, *The State of Alaska;* Bob Henning, Editor, *The Milepost;* Aurel Krause, *The Tlingit Indians;* George Laycock, *Alaska: The Embattled Frontier;* Robert Marshall, *Alaska Wilderness: Exploring the Central Brooks Range;* Elaine Mitchell, Editor, *Alaska Blue Book 1975;* Murray Morgan, *One Man's Gold Rush: A Klondike Album;* Donald J. Orth, *Dictionary of Alaska Place Names;* David A. Remley, *Crooked Road: The Story of the Alaska Highway;* George W. Rogers, *Change in Alaska;* Archie Satterfield, *The Chilkoot Pass: Then and Now;* David B. Wharton, *The Alaska Gold Rush.* National Geographic Special Publication: Bern Keating, *Alaska.* In NATIONAL GEOGRAPHIC: William S. Ellis, "North Slope: Will Alaska's Oil and Tundra Mix?" October 1971; Bryan Hodgson, "The Pipeline: Alaska's Troubled Colossus," November 1976; Joseph Judge, "Alaska: Rising Northern Star," June 1975; Emory Kristof, "The Last U. S. Whale Hunters," March 1973; Jim Rearden, "A Bit of Old Russia Takes Root in Alaska," September 1972; "A Look at Alaska's Tundra," March 1972. Readers may also wish to consult the National Geographic Index for related material.

Library of Congress CIP Data

National Geographic Society,
  Washington, D. C. Special Pub-
  lications Division.
  Alaska: High Roads to Adventure.

  Bibliography: p. 198.
  Includes index.
  1. Alaska—Description and travel—
1959-
F910.N37   979.8'05   76-692
ISBN 0-87044-193-0

Composition for *Alaska: High Roads to Adventure* by National Geographic's Photo-
graphic Services, Carl M. Shrader, Chief; Lawrence F. Ludwig, Assistant Chief.
Printed and bound by Kingsport Press, Kingsport, Tenn. Color separations by Beck
Engraving Co., Philadelphia, Pa.; Colorgraphics, Inc., Beltsville, Md.; Graphic Color
Plate, Inc., Stamford, Conn.; Progressive Color Corp., Rockville, Md.; J. Wm. Reed
Co., Alexandria, Va.